Advance Praise for
Building Your Board of Directors for Life

"Excellent, original concept, very clearly explained. Putting together a personal cabinet of advisors is a surefire recipe for success in one's career and life. Dennis Baker has hit upon something seemingly simple yet profoundly impactful."

—**Barbara Greenleaf,** author of the "Business-Minded Teens" books, former *New York Times* journalist

"This book is a transformative guide to building meaningful relationships that propel personal and professional success. The insights and actionable steps are invaluable for anyone looking to grow through mentorship."

—**Lisa Kristine,** world-renowned photographer and humanitarian, founder of the Human Thread Foundation

"Dennis Baker provides a clear and engaging roadmap for creating a lifelong network of trusted advisors—an invaluable asset. This book is a testament to the power of mentorship and servant leadership."

—**Ben Everard,** attorney, movie producer, Gray Matter Studios, Everard Entertainment

"*Building Your Board of Directors for Life* is a must-read for everyone! The powerful lessons in this book equip the reader to live a truly successful life. Dennis Baker is an extraordinary leader who teaches by example."

—**Kathy Ireland,** supermodel, entrepreneur, CEO, Kathy Ireland Worldwide

"I wholeheartedly recommend this remarkable volume by Dennis Baker, who has chosen a fascinating and innovative idea, and gone on to explain it in a very understandable way. The book is infused with and based on a truly original idea, designed for everyone's individual needs and circumstances. Dennis has provided both a guide and advice on how to improve and enrich your journey through life, and to maximize your potential, navigating the complexities, superficiality, and short-termism of so much of society today. But this is no theoretical work. Throughout the book, Dennis has drawn on his own very wide life experiences and observations to construct a plan for others based on the practicalities of what he himself has been part of, and what he has achieved, and then done an extraordinary job of drawing together all the various threads into a lifelong plan."

—**Alan Amos,** former Member of Parliament,
former Lord Mayor of Worcester, England

"CEO and entrepreneur Dennis Baker's new book is a literal roadmap on how to surround yourself with people and mentors you can trust, who have your best interests at heart and will help you reach your full career potential. A must-read, period."

—**Wendy Whitman,** former VP of CourtTV,
attorney, producer, author

"Dennis Baker delivers a truly transformative guide that empowers you to cultivate meaningful relationships with those who inspire, challenge, and elevate your life. This is an invaluable resource for anyone striving for personal and professional growth."

—**Rita Cosby,** Emmy-winning TV host/journalist,
bestselling author

"A masterclass in mentorship and leadership, this book is a must-read for anyone looking to build meaningful relationships that inspire growth and success."

—**Adam Caplan,** venture capitalist,
Jumpspace Ventures

"Show me a successful person in a leadership position and I'll bet they had some mentorship along the way. No matter how self-assured or confident, most of us could benefit from guidance at some point in our lives. But forming and cultivating those relationships is a skill. Dennis Baker shows you how to assemble that coveted team of advisors and mentors to help you reach your highest potential."

—**Gene Lim,** CEO, MAV-12,
entrepreneur, producer, strategist

"In cultures around the world, the wisdom of elders is revered. In Dennis Baker's book *Building Your Board of Directors for Life*, he offers a how-to guide to finding your circle of elders. There's an African saying, 'When we go alone, we go fast. When we go together, we go far.' This book equips the reader to go far with the wisdom and lived experience of a group of trusted advisors."

—**Casey Rogers,** founder and CEO,
Telea Insights, The Ellen Fund

"Why do some people thrive at meaningful connections while others fail? In this book, Dennis Baker teaches that building connections is a learned skill, making *Building Your Board of Directors for Life* the most useful call to action since Dale Carnegie's *How to Win Friends and Influence People*."

—**Morgan Murphy,** US Navy Captain,
former Pentagon spokesperson

"In a world where relationships are everything, this book provides the clarity and strategy to build your inner circle of champions."

—**Cat Greenleaf,** founder of The Restorative Housing Organization, former *Today Show* personality (NBC's *Talk Stoop*)

"Dennis Baker knows the value of mentorship from his prized personal 'board of directors' and from truly serving on 'boards' for many of his own mentees. He takes this concept far beyond professional to a higher goal of personal betterment on all levels, as we learn from those who have gone before us, and as we now make an impact and leave a legacy for those whom we help come up in the world. This is an inspiring read for all of us in any field."

—**Doug Jones,** actor, *Pan's Labyrinth, The Shape of Water, Hellboy, Star Trek*: *Discovery*

BUILDING YOUR BOARD OF DIRECTORS FOR LIFE

BUILDING YOUR BOARD OF DIRECTORS FOR LIFE

Create a Network That Guides, Supports, and Inspires You

Dennis M. Baker

Post Hill Press

A POST HILL PRESS BOOK
ISBN: 979-8-89565-259-6
ISBN (eBook): 979-8-89565-260-2

Building Your Board of Directors for Life:
Create a Network That Guides, Supports, and Inspires You

Cover design by Jim Villaflores
Cover concept by Brian Buffon

This book, as well as any other Post Hill Press publications, may be purchased in bulk quantities at a special discounted rate. Contact orders@posthillpress.com for more information.

Although every effort has been made to ensure that the personal and professional advice present within this book is useful and appropriate, the author and publisher do not assume and hereby disclaim any liability to any person, business, or organization choosing to employ the guidance offered in this book.

This is a work of nonfiction. All people, locations, events, and situations are portrayed to the best of the author's memory.

Post Hill
PRESS

Post Hill Press
New York • Nashville
posthillpress.com

Published in the United States of America
1 2 3 4 5 6 7 8 9 10

*To the Lord, who has been my Counselor, Mentor,
and the steady voice behind every good decision.*

CONTENTS

FOREWORD

MENTORSHIP IS NOT JUST A CONCEPT but a way of life for my mentor and friend, Dennis Baker. Divine intervention is the best way I can explain what brought him into my life while I was in high school, through circumstances that seem uncanny. We initially met over coffee to discuss a completely unrelated matter, but it didn't take long for my interest to shift towards his business acumen and sharp insights. Driven by curiosity, I asked if I could "tag along" with him for a workday, hoping to learn more, and he graciously agreed. That moment marked the beginning of my first direct mentor-mentee relationship.

Over the next year and a half, Dennis became more than just a mentor—he became the "chairman of the board" on my personal board of directors. I looked to him not only for guidance but also as an example of what it means to lead with purpose and discipline. I was so inspired by the work we were doing that I asked Dennis if I could drop out of Cal Poly San Luis Obispo to join him full-time at his Los Angeles–based tech start-up.

Being the responsible man that he is, Dennis didn't want me to prioritize short-term goals over my long-term success. He agreed to let me work with him only if I stayed in college and continued my education. Begrudgingly, I followed his advice and transferred to a Community College in Los Angeles, balancing a full course load while gaining hands-on experience learning about the start-up world. As I proved my value and became more of an asset to Dennis, I was given increasingly more responsibility. Eventually, I was part of Dennis's pitch team to investors and found myself dealing with almost every aspect of the start-up from marketing to investor relationships to cap tables. I learned a great deal in the process and became an equity partner along the way. I can confidently say that I learned more about business and leadership working alongside Dennis than I ever did in a classroom.

As I grew, our relationship deepened from mentorship into a true friendship, and eventually into a brotherhood. Dennis's ability to build and maintain his own board of directors, and to use those relationships to guide and serve others, is the foundation of what makes him an extraordinary servant leader.

The most profound example of this came in 2018 when my life took an unexpected turn. I was in a car accident that left me with a traumatic brain injury (TBI), an impairment with a long and delicate recovery process (along with many other injuries). I was unable to drive, cook, or even be left alone for fear that I might forget where I was or what I was doing. Dennis stepped in immediately, putting aside the business we had built together to dedicate himself to my care. He took on everything—paying my rent and credit card bills, ensuring I had the support I needed in my day-to-day life, and even investigating my case, securing legal representation, and making sure I was protected.

Dennis didn't do this alone. He reached out to his own board of directors, seeking advice from legal, medical, and practical experts to navigate my recovery. With Dennis's help and my medical team, I was able to make a miraculous recovery. Time and again, Dennis leveraged his network not only for his own success but also to serve others in their time of need.

Even today, Dennis remains one of the first people I turn to when I need advice. If he doesn't have the answer himself, he knows exactly where to find it. He has even gone so far as to connect me directly with members of his board of directors when it was necessary.

Having had the privilege of reading this book, I can say without hesitation that Dennis is uniquely qualified to speak on the topic of mentorship and building your own Board of Directors for Life. He lives these principles every day, and his unwavering commitment to helping others achieve their potential is what makes him such an inspiring leader.

Dennis has been a mentor, a friend, and a guide in my life, and I have no doubt will become the same for you as you read this book and put its wisdom into practice.

—R. Kurt Gabriel

INTRODUCTION

BUILDING A PERSONAL BOARD OF DIRECTORS FOR *LIFE*

WHAT IF SUCCESS WASN'T MEANT to be a solo journey? What if the secret to making better decisions, navigating challenges, and unlocking opportunities lay not in going it alone but in surrounding yourself with the right people?

Imagine having your own personal board of directors—a group of trusted mentors offering guidance, support, and perspective when you need it most. What if this network could help you see possibilities you hadn't considered, push you to grow in ways you never imagined, and hold you accountable to your highest potential? What if having the right people in your corner could not only accelerate your progress but also provide the clarity and confidence you need to take bold steps forward?

In today's complex and often isolating world, it's easy to feel stuck, uncertain, or disconnected. Despite the many ways we can connect through technology, research shows that feelings of loneliness and lack of direction are at an all-time high. We are more "connected" than ever, yet many struggle to find meaningful guidance and support in their personal and professional lives. Could it be that we've lost something fundamental—the deep, intentional relationships that once helped us find our way?

The truth is anyone can build a network of mentors—a diverse group of advisors who offer insight, encouragement, and practical wisdom. But how do you find the right people? How do you cultivate these relationships in a way that is authentic and mutually beneficial? How do you ensure that your personal board evolves with you, adapting to new challenges and aspirations as you grow?

This book is your guide to answering those questions. It's about more than just mentorship; it's about creating a dynamic support system that serves as both a safety net and a springboard, offering stability in times of uncertainty and propelling you forward when opportunity arises. A board of directors for your life isn't about relinquishing control; it's about expanding your perspective, sharpening your decision-making, and ensuring that you're never facing critical choices alone.

Whether you're navigating your career, making a major life decision, or simply trying to figure out what's next, the right mentors can change everything. They can challenge you, champion you, and provide the wisdom you might not yet have but desperately need. The question isn't whether mentorship matters—it's whether you're ready to embrace it as a *strategic* advantage.

Are you willing to build the relationships that could change your trajectory? Are you ready to create your personal Board of Directors for Life? If so, let's go!

CHAPTER 1

A BRIEF HISTORY OF MENTORSHIP

- **A brief history:** The concept of mentorship dates to ancient civilizations, where knowledge was passed down from experienced leaders to the next generation through structured guidance.

THE LOST ART OF MENTORSHIP

In today's world, where life moves faster than ever and demands on our time and energy feel relentless, the importance of good advice has only grown. We live in a culture that often idolizes independence and self-sufficiency to the point of isolation. The pressure to achieve, stay relevant, and navigate increasingly complex personal and professional landscapes can leave us feeling overwhelmed and unsure of the best path forward. This is where mentors-trusted advisors who provide guidance, support, and accountability—can make all the difference.

Now imagine having not just one advisor, but several. How much better, more diverse, and exceptional would your decision-making and growth be if you had an entire team of advisors to turn to? Throughout this book, I'll take you behind the scenes of my own journey—sharing pivotal moments that unfolded because I had a board of directors behind me. You'll hear how seemingly casual introductions turned into life-changing opportunities, how the right guidance helped me bounce back from a public loss, and how mentorship opened doors in business, politics, and beyond that I never would've reached alone. Each chapter unveils a new layer—not just of mentorship in action, but of the strategic moves and authentic relationships that shaped who I've become.

These stories aren't just highlights—they're proof that when you surround yourself with the right people, your life expands in unexpected and powerful ways. You'll meet CEOs, celebrities, politicians, and everyday heroes who poured into me—and you'll learn how to find and connect with mentors who can do the same for you. Consider this your personal blueprint for building something far more valuable than a résumé: a purpose-driven network that evolves with you, challenges you, and helps you become the person you're meant to be.

A Brief History

Mentorship itself is not new. For centuries, it has been the foundation of personal and professional growth across cultures and eras. Whether in formal relationships, like apprenticeships, or informal ones where wisdom is passed down from elder to younger, mentorship has consistently helped individuals face life's challenges. The modern trend of undervaluing the guidance of mentors or elders—treating them as optional—is unique to recent history and doesn't reflect the enduring role of mentorship in human development.

The concept of "mentorship" has ancient roots. It first appeared in Homer's *Odyssey*, where **Mentor** was a character entrusted by Odysseus to guide his son, Telemachus. Eventually, "mentor" came to refer to someone who provides advice, support, and guidance—particularly in professional or educational contexts. This tradition, dating back to the twelfth century BCE, underscores how deeply mentorship is woven into the fabric of human progress.

One of history's most famous mentorships was the relationship between Aristotle and Alexander the Great. **Aristotle,** who had been mentored by **Plato** (a student of **Socrates**), passed down not only philosophical insights but also critical-thinking and strategic skills. These equipped Alexander to become one of history's greatest military leaders and thinkers. Aristotle's guidance shaped not only Alexander's path but also the course of history, illustrating the transformative power of mentorship.

Mentorship also played a central role in medieval Europe through the guild systems. These guilds—associations of artisans and merchants—did much more than regulate trade and craftsmanship. They offered a structured path for skill development, from apprenticeship to journeyman to master craftsman. This hierarchy fostered mentorship at every level, with experienced masters passing down their knowledge and techniques. Beyond economic support, guilds created strong community bonds, providing help to members during times of need and even participating in local governance. Although guilds faded with industrialization, their legacy lives on in modern professional organizations and apprenticeship programs.

CLIENT-PATRON RELATIONSHIPS IN AFRICA AND TURN-OF-THE-CENTURY BOSTON: A MENTORSHIP PERSPECTIVE

Throughout history, client-patron relationships have played a big role in shaping how people get ahead in society. In many African communities, these relationships are built on mutual support between powerful figures—like chiefs, elders, or wealthy individuals—and those who rely on them for resources, protection, or opportunities. Patrons provide guidance, financial help, or political backing, and in return, their clients show loyalty, work for them, or support them in their leadership roles. These relationships are deeply rooted in tradition and kinship, often serving as a form of mentorship where experienced individuals help others navigate life and advance in society.

In turn-of-the-century Boston, a similar dynamic played out, especially under the influence of **John "Honey" Fitzgerald.** As a major political figure (longtime mayor of Boston) and the grandfather of future president John F. Kennedy, Fitzgerald gained his power by offering jobs, social services, and opportunities to working-class immigrants—particularly the Irish—in exchange for their loyalty and votes. Boston's political machine operated through this kind of patronage system, where rising politicians and community leaders got their start by aligning with powerful figures who could open doors for them. In many ways, this was an early form of mentorship, where guidance and support were given, but with the expectation of loyalty and future favors in return.

Both African patronage systems and Boston's political networks show how mentorship has historically been tied to access and opportunity. While today's idea of mentorship tends to focus more on personal and professional growth without the expectation of returning favors, these older systems were often transactional. Still, the core idea remains the same—having someone more experienced help guide the way can make all the difference in a person's ability to succeed. Looking at these historical relationships gives us a better understanding of how mentorship has evolved into a more structured, equitable, and ethical system, one that ideally focuses on mutual growth rather than obligation.

Mentorship isn't limited to practical or professional guidance. It also holds a profound place in faith traditions. Though this book isn't, in nature, religious, I would be remiss as a Christian if I didn't acknowledge the influence of mentorship examples from the Bible. Figures like **Jesus, Moses, Elijah, and Barnabas** exemplified the impact of guiding others, shaping successors who carried their legacies forward. For example, Barnabas mentored the apostle Paul, supporting and advocating for him as he became a key leader in the early Christian community. Barnabas's encouragement helped Paul find his footing, develop his skills, and eventually make a lasting impact, writing nearly half of the New Testament. This story highlights how mentorship is about building potential and guiding others toward their purpose.

This tradition of mentorship as a personal and transformative relationship is as relevant today as it was centuries ago. The best mentorship relationships go beyond short-term advice. They are built for the long haul, providing the connection, accountability, and insight necessary to shape lives and drive success. In these relationships, fine-tuning occurs over time, creating a lasting impact. It's akin to a rocket launch to the moon—tiny deviations at takeoff can result in being hundreds or thousands of miles off course, significantly affecting the trajectory and your ability to reach your destination. Likewise, not making course corrections incrementally—one degree this way, one degree that—can leave you far off course down the line. Great advice doesn't just help you succeed; it gives you the trajectory you need to reach your desired destination in life.

Historically, mentorship has shaped leaders, scientists, and innovators. Many influential figures benefited from mentorship, whether through formal or informal relationships. Here are some notable examples:

16th Century

**Queen Elizabeth I (1533–1603)—
Mentored by William Cecil**

- Elizabeth relied on William Cecil, her chief advisor, for political and strategic counsel throughout her reign. His mentorship helped her navigate complex international relations and solidify her legacy as one of England's greatest monarchs.

17th Century

**Isaac Newton (1642–1727)—
Mentored by Isaac Barrow**

- Newton, one of history's greatest scientists, was mentored by Isaac Barrow, a mathematician and theologian who recognized Newton's talent and helped him secure a position at Cambridge.

**John Locke (1632–1704)—
Mentored by Lord Ashley (Earl of Shaftesbury)**

- The philosopher John Locke was mentored by Anthony Ashley Cooper, the 1st Earl of Shaftesbury, who introduced him to politics and philosophy, shaping his ideas on government and human rights.

18th Century

**Benjamin Franklin (1706–1790)—
Mentored by James Franklin and later Sir William Keith**

- Franklin was first mentored by his older brother James in the printing trade, then later received guidance from Sir William Keith, the governor of Pennsylvania, though Keith's uncertain support led Franklin to become more self-reliant.

Napoleon Bonaparte (1769–1821)—Mentored by Maximilien Robespierre's brother, Augustin

- During the French Revolution, Napoleon gained favor and military opportunities through his association with Augustin Robespierre, who helped advance his early career.

Adam Smith (1723–1790)—Mentored by David Hume

- The Scottish economist Adam Smith was greatly influenced by philosopher David Hume, whose ideas helped shape Smith's seminal work, *The Wealth of Nations.*

19th Century

Abraham Lincoln (1809–1865)—Mentored by Joshua Speed and William Mentor Graham

- Lincoln's early intellectual development was influenced by William Mentor Graham, a schoolteacher. Later, Joshua Speed, a businessman, became a close confidant who helped him navigate political and personal challenges.

Frederick Douglass (1818–1895)—Mentored by William Lloyd Garrison

- The abolitionist Frederick Douglass was mentored by William Lloyd Garrison, who helped promote his writing and speaking career, boosting his influence in the antislavery movement.

Booker T. Washington (1856–1915)— Mentored by Samuel Chapman Armstrong

- Washington, a leader in African American education, was mentored by Samuel Chapman Armstrong, the founder of Hampton Normal and Agricultural Institute, who helped him establish Tuskegee University.

Theodore Roosevelt (1858–1919) — Mentored by Henry Cabot Lodge

- Roosevelt benefited from the mentorship of Henry Cabot Lodge, a U.S. senator who helped shape his political career and guided him in foreign policy matters.

Thomas Edison (1847–1931)— Mentored by Franklin Leonard Pope

- As a young inventor, Edison was guided by Franklin Leonard Pope, an engineer and editor who helped him gain practical experience and business connections.

20th Century

Franklin D. Roosevelt (1882–1945)— Mentored by Woodrow Wilson and Louis Howe

- FDR was influenced by President Woodrow Wilson early in his career and later received invaluable political guidance from his advisor Louis Howe, his closest political strategist and surrogate.

John F. Kennedy (1917–1963)—Mentored by Joseph P. Kennedy Sr. and Richard Nixon (early on)

- JFK was heavily influenced by his father, Joseph Kennedy Sr., who guided his political ambitions. Early in his career, he also learned from Richard Nixon before they became political rivals. (Surprised by that one, I bet.)

Martin Luther King Jr. (1929–1968)—Mentored by Benjamin Mays

- King was profoundly shaped by Benjamin Mays, the president of Morehouse College, who instilled in him the values of nonviolent protest and social justice.

Walt Disney (1901–1966)—Mentored by Ub Iwerks

- Disney's early animation career was supported by Ub Iwerks, a fellow animator who played a key role in the creation of Mickey Mouse and helped Disney refine his artistic skills.

Margaret Thatcher (1925–2013)—Mentored by Keith Joseph

- Thatcher, the first female prime minister of the United Kingdom, was mentored by Keith Joseph, a Conservative politician and key architect of Thatcherism. His economic philosophies and political guidance helped shape her approach to free-market policies and leadership.

It's nearly impossible to find leaders or innovators who were not mentored by others and whose guidance influenced them and the world we know.

Chapter Challenge: Who from history was especially inspiring to you? What attributes did you admire most?

Then let us know what you learned so far with the following hashtags:

Instagram, Substack and X @yourboard4life
#chapter1challenge #yourboard4life

CHAPTER 2

THE NEED FOR MENTORSHIP—WHY IT MATTERS

- **Benefits of mentorship:** Guidance, connection, growth, confidence, accountability.
- **Historic and contemporary case studies:** Visionaries like Abraham Lincoln, Steve Jobs, Warren Buffett, and Winston Churchill all benefited from influential mentors who shaped their leadership, innovation, and decision-making skills.
- **My journey:** How eighty-six votes paved the way to building my personal board

WHY MENTORSHIP MATTERS

In an era marked by rapid technological advancement, the need for mentorship has never been more crucial. The sheer volume of data available today is staggering. However, sifting through this information to find meaningful, actionable insights can be overwhelming. This is where mentorship shines, offering guidance and the clarity needed to navigate life's complexities effectively. And when mentorship is at its best, it is built around a servant leadership approach by both mentor and mentee.

Having a mentor offers several benefits:

- **Guidance and Advice:** Mentors can provide valuable guidance and advice based on their experiences and knowledge, helping you navigate challenges and decisions in your career or personal life.
- **Skill Development:** Mentors can help you identify and develop critical skills for career growth or personal development. They can offer insights into areas where you need improvement and suggest ways to enhance these skills.
- **Connection Opportunities:** Mentors often introduce their mentees to professional networks, opening doors to new opportunities, connections, and resources that might otherwise be difficult to access.
- **Increased Confidence:** Receiving support and encouragement from a mentor may make you feel more confident in your abilities and decisions. This can be particularly valuable when facing new challenges or stepping out of your comfort zone, and it gives you access to an objective point of view of yourself from an experienced outside source.
- **Goal Setting and Accountability:** Mentors can help you set realistic goals and provide accountability, helping you stay focused and motivated to achieve them.
- **Career Advancement:** Mentors can provide insights into career progression, including advice on promotions, job changes, and industry dynamics, which can be crucial for advancing in your

career and helping avoid critical mistakes that could hinder your advancement.

- **Personal Growth:** Beyond professional development, mentors can also contribute to personal growth by encouraging self-reflection, providing emotional support, and helping you understand your personal strengths and weaknesses.
- **Broader Perspectives:** A mentor can offer a different perspective and help you see situations in a new light, which can be invaluable in problem-solving and personal development.
- **Inspiration and Motivation:** Mentors often serve as role models, inspiring you to reach your full potential and motivating you through their own success stories and perseverance as well as cheering you on as you write your own.

FEEDBACK AND CONSTRUCTIVE CRITICISM

Receiving honest and constructive feedback from someone you trust and respect can be incredibly beneficial for personal and professional growth. Mentorship offers a unique space where this kind of guidance thrives, helping individuals improve and reach new heights.

Mentorship has a rich history and continues to evolve. Its impact can be seen in the development of leaders, the advancement of knowledge, and the progress of societies. Throughout history, the relationships between mentors and mentees have formed a tapestry of shared wisdom and achievement.

SUPPORT: BUILDING RESILIENCE IN TIMES OF UNCERTAINTY

Having advisors isn't just about feedback and critique—it's also about support, both emotional and practical. Life is unpredictable, and the journey to success is rarely straightforward. Having someone in your corner who genuinely cares about your growth can make all the difference, especially during challenging times.

Winston Churchill benefited greatly from two key figures—**David Lloyd George** and **Bourke Cockran**—playing pivotal roles in shaping his personal and professional development. These relationships helped mold Churchill into the leader who would guide Britain through its darkest hours in World War II.

David Lloyd George, a prominent British statesman and one of Churchill's seniors in the early twentieth century, was instrumental in helping Churchill navigate the complexities of political life. Their bond grew stronger during World War I when Lloyd George, then prime minister, brought Churchill back into government in 1917 after the Gallipoli Campaign—a disaster that had tarnished Churchill's reputation. By appointing Churchill as minister of munitions, Lloyd George not only demonstrated his belief in Churchill's abilities but also helped him regain his footing in government and rebuild his career.

Lloyd George's mentorship went beyond career restoration. He also influenced Churchill's views on progressive social policies. Both men shared roots in the Liberal Party and a commitment to addressing poverty and working-class issues. Lloyd George's People's Budget of 1909, which introduced fair taxation and social welfare programs, deeply inspired Churchill's later efforts in domestic reform.

More than that, Lloyd George taught Churchill the art of political pragmatism. As a master coalition builder, Lloyd George demonstrated how to unite opposing parties in times of national crisis, such as during World War I when he brought Liberals and Conservatives together. Churchill, who later became a Conservative, would draw on these lessons when he led a coalition government during World War II, transcending party politics. Lloyd George's resilience in the face of opposition and ability to survive political storms were lessons Churchill internalized, becoming key aspects of his leadership.

Across the Atlantic, Churchill found another key mentor in Bourke Cockran, an Irish-American politician celebrated for his powerful oratory and independent thinking. Churchill first met Cockran during his visits to the United States in the early 1900s. Captivated by Cockran's ability to inspire audiences with his eloquent speeches, Churchill recognized that mastering public speaking would be crucial to his political career. Eager to learn, he adopted many of Cockran's techniques, such as the strategic use of pauses, cadence, and emphasis, to make his speeches more impactful.

Cockran's influence extended beyond public speaking. Their discussions touched on leadership, democracy, and the responsibilities of those in power. Cockran's emphasis on moral clarity and conviction resonated deeply with Churchill, providing a philosophical foundation that would guide him as he navigated the turbulent political landscape of the twentieth century.

Churchill often reflected on Cockran's teachings, particularly during the 1930s when he became one of the few vocal critics of Adolf Hitler's rise to power. Cockran had reinforced the importance of standing firm against tyranny and valuing democratic principles, lessons that bolstered Churchill as he warned against appeasement and advocated for decisive action.

The combined guidance of Lloyd George and Bourke Cockran helped Churchill become the leader who inspired a nation during its darkest hours. Lloyd George's lessons in political strategy, resilience, and social reform gave Churchill the tools to navigate government complexities, while Cockran's mentorship in public speaking and conviction equipped him to rally a nation and its allies.

Churchill's legendary wartime speeches, including "We Shall Fight on the Beaches" and "Their Finest Hour," reflected Cockran's influence in their delivery and moral strength. Together, the lessons from these two mentors shaped Churchill's approach to leadership, leaving an enduring legacy as one of the most remarkable figures in history.

This highlights how even a few lifelong mentors with different skill sets can provide transformative guidance, proving that mentorship isn't just a tool for success—it's a foundation for resilience and greatness.

GUIDANCE: NAVIGATING THROUGH CHANGE

Of course, one of the most valuable benefits of having a mentor is their ability to provide guidance, especially during times of change. In today's workplaces, employees often juggle multiple responsibilities, adapt to emerging technologies, and stay ahead of rapidly shifting industry trends. Without someone to offer perspective, it's easy to feel overwhelmed or make choices that may not align with long-term goals.

For example, imagine a young professional starting out in the tech industry. They might feel unsure about which programming languages to prioritize, which projects to focus on, or how to prepare for future leadership roles. An experienced mentor in their field can step in to offer clarity, sharing insights about the most impactful skills and how to develop them. This kind of tailored guidance not only saves time but also helps the mentee avoid common pitfalls and make thoughtful decisions that support their career aspirations. Finding an advocate within a company or organization can be an invaluable resource.

In the corporate world, a mentor's support can mean the difference between success and failure. A recent *Forbes* article, "The Power of Mentorship: How Mentors Can Help Employees Grow and Succeed," emphasized the importance of mentorship in navigating change. Corporate mentorship programs are powerful tools for fostering growth and helping employees adjust to new challenges. Mentors provide emotional support during uncertain times, equipping mentees with the tools and perspectives they need to adapt to evolving roles and industry trends. This support helps employees manage stress, build resilience, and develop innovative approaches to problem-solving.

Mentorship also plays a key role in creating inclusive and collaborative workplaces. By fostering a sense of connection and alignment, mentors help teams work together more effectively and prepare for challenges as a cohesive unit. In essence, mentors act as a guiding compass, aligning personal growth with organizational goals while addressing the demands of a constantly changing world.

While building mentorship relationships within a corporate structure is highly encouraged and serves an important purpose, it's just as crucial to seek mentors outside the workplace. External mentors can provide a broader perspective and offer advice that is free from the potential conflicts of interest that may arise in a corporate setting. This balanced approach ensures you receive well-rounded guidance that aligns with both your professional ambitions and personal values.

ACCOUNTABILITY: TURNING INTENTIONS INTO ACTIONS

While support and guidance are essential, accountability is often the key to turning good intentions into meaningful actions. We all have goals—whether they involve advancing in our careers, growing personally, or making a difference in our communities. But without someone to hold us accountable, it's all too easy to lose focus, get sidetracked, or even abandon those aspirations altogether.

A great example of accountability in a relationship is between Warren Buffett and his mentor, **Benjamin Graham,** a British-born American financial analyst, investor, economist, and professor widely known as the "father of value investing." Today, Buffett is one of the most successful investors in the world, and he often credits Graham for shaping his investment philosophy. But their relationship wasn't just about passing on financial wisdom; Graham held Buffett accountable to the high standards they set together, ensuring he maintained the discipline needed to succeed.

Graham's tutelage went beyond teaching Buffett how to analyze stocks. It was about guiding him to think critically and make decisions with long-term goals in mind. When Buffett felt tempted to stray from his principles, he remembered Graham's advice about staying true to the bigger picture. This accountability helped Buffett avoid short-term distractions and stay true to the value-investing strategies that ultimately defined his career. Without Graham's steady influence, Buffett's path might have looked very different.

In corporate settings, mentorship programs also emphasize accountability as a cornerstone of professional development. Many organizations pair new employees with seasoned mentors who help them set goals and create actionable plans. These mentors regularly check in, offering feedback and keeping mentees on track to achieve their objectives. This kind of accountability accelerates personal growth and fosters a culture of continuous improvement within the organization.

Accountability isn't just about checking off tasks—it's about encouraging a commitment to excellence and long-term growth. It helps transform dreams into actionable plans, keeping individuals focused and motivated. Whether in investing, business, or personal development, having a mentor who provides accountability can be the difference between merely dreaming and truly achieving.

Mentors, however, need to know you to truly hold you accountable. While we can learn from public figures, online platforms, and inspirational leaders, these sources can't tailor their advice to your unique circumstances. It's important to cultivate relationships with real, present advisors who understand your specific needs, aspirations, and challenges.

SOLVING CHALLENGES THROUGH MENTORSHIP

Many people face challenges that hinder personal and professional growth. One of the most common is decision paralysis, also known as "analysis paralysis"—the inability to choose a direction when overwhelmed with too many options. It's easy to get stuck in analysis and miss opportunities. A mentor can be a game changer in breaking this cycle by offering clarity and perspective.

Take, for instance, a young professional facing several career paths, each with its own risks and rewards. Without guidance, they might feel immobilized by fear of making the wrong decision. A mentor, drawing from their own experience, can help weigh the pros and cons, offer insights into potential outcomes tailored to the person, and ultimately guide them toward a confident choice. This kind of mentorship not only reduces stress but also provides a clear direction forward.

Another common challenge is a lack of direction. Feeling uncertain about which path to take—whether in your career, personal life, or daily decisions—can be paralyzing, especially during times of transition. An advisor helps provide focus by helping you set clear, achievable goals and creating a strategy to reach them.

Take the example of Thomas Edison, one of the greatest inventors in history. Early in his career, he was mentored by telegraph pioneer **Franklin Leonard Pope,** who provided technical guidance and business insights. Pope's mentorship helped Edison focus his creative energy, turning him from a tinkerer into a prolific inventor with over one thousand patents. With Pope's direction, and later with the help of financiers like J.P. Morgan and Henry Ford, Edison's genius was fully actualized.

Feeling overwhelmed is yet another challenge many face today. Between work, personal responsibilities, and societal expectations, it's easy to feel isolated and stressed. Mentors can help by providing perspective and helping prioritize what truly matters.

For example, President Abraham Lincoln faced immense pressure during the Civil War. He often turned to his secretary of state, **William Seward,** (a former rival) for advice. Seward's political experience and steady support helped Lincoln prioritize critical issues and manage the overwhelming responsibilities of leading a nation at war. Their partnership gave Lincoln the resilience to carry on during the war's most difficult moments.

Mentorship is much more than just solving problems—it's about growth, self-discovery, and purpose. It provides clarity when faced with indecision, direction when you feel lost, and encouragement when you're overwhelmed. Most importantly, mentorship gives you the confidence that someone is invested in your success, motivating you to reach higher and push beyond your limits.

MENTORS: THE HIDDEN FORCE BEHIND INNOVATION AND LEADERSHIP

Steve Jobs, the visionary cofounder of Apple, similarly benefited from a series of mentors and influential figures who shaped his innovative and entrepreneurial journey. Each relationship contributed in unique ways to his groundbreaking approach to technology and business.

Cabinets and Kitchen Cabinets

U.S. presidents often rely on trusted advisors outside of their formal cabinets. These individuals, sometimes referred to as a "kitchen cabinet," are a select group of personal confidants who have often been part of the president's life long before their White House tenure. This informal group is unique because they know the president deeply, understanding blind spots, biases, and personal history. The trustworthiness built over years allows them to provide the kind of unvarnished opinions that even the most formal advisors might hesitate to give.

One of Jobs's earliest influences was **Robert Friedland,** an entrepreneurial and charismatic figure he met at Reed College. Friedland encouraged Jobs to explore creative, unconventional ideas and embrace bold thinking—what would later become Apple's iconic "Think Different" ethos. Their conversations inspired Jobs's passion for merging technology with business and instilled in him a willingness to challenge the status quo. This foundational mentorship profoundly shaped Jobs's entrepreneurial vision as he launched his career.

Another key figure in Jobs's early years was **Nolan Bushnell,** the co-founder of Atari. After leaving college, Jobs joined Atari, where he learned invaluable lessons about design, technology, and business. Bushnell's focus on creating user-centered, engaging experiences inspired Jobs to pursue his vision of building products that blended artistic elegance with functional practicality. Bushnell's mentorship emphasized the importance of intuitive design and creating technology that resonated with people on an emotional level—principles that would later define Apple's philosophy.

As Apple took shape, **Mike Markkula,** an early investor, became a crucial mentor. Markkula provided strategic guidance on marketing and business operations, teaching Jobs the importance of understanding customers and building a sustainable enterprise. His mentorship during Apple's formative years helped Jobs navigate the complexities of the tech world and laid the groundwork for Apple's emergence as a revolutionary brand.

Jobs also collaborated closely with **Andy Hertzfeld,** a key member of the original Macintosh development team. Hertzfeld's technical expertise and creative problem-solving skills were instrumental in advancing the Macintosh project. Jobs valued Hertzfeld's perspective and fostered a collaborative environment that emphasized innovation and teamwork. Their partnership highlighted Jobs's ability to nurture talent and cultivate a culture of excellence.

Another notable influence was **John Sculley,** the former CEO of PepsiCo, whom Jobs recruited to lead Apple in 1983. Initially,

Sculley provided mentorship in managing a large corporation and navigating complex business dynamics. Although their relationship later turned contentious, with Sculley eventually ousting Jobs from Apple, the experience taught Jobs critical lessons about leadership and resilience. These lessons shaped his approach when he returned to Apple years later, leading the company to unprecedented success.

Through these relationships, Jobs developed a distinctive approach to leadership, creativity, and innovation that reshaped the technology landscape. His journey—shaped by Friedland, Bushnell, Markkula, Hertzfeld, and Sculley—demonstrates how mentorship fuels ambition and growth. Each mentor left an indelible mark on Jobs's legacy, contributing to the visionary entrepreneur who forever changed the world of technology and design.

MY JOURNEY

When I was a teenager, I came across Proverbs 15:22, "Without counsel plans fail, but with many advisors, they succeed." That simple truth resonated deeply with me. Even at a young age, I understood that finding clarity and solving problems is rarely a solitary pursuit.

Building your personal board of mentors begins with identifying the right people: those who are experienced, ethical, and invested in your growth. It's not just about finding successful individuals; it's about finding mentors who align with your specific needs and aspirations. These are people who see your potential and are willing to help you reach it.

Once you've identified potential advisors, the next step is nurturing those relationships. Building a personal board requires mutual respect, consistent communication, and genuine appreciation. You must be authentic. When these relationships are cultivated thoughtfully, they provide the foundation for lasting support and guidance throughout your life.

The true power of your board lies in leveraging their collective wisdom. Whether you're navigating a career transition, resolving a personal dilemma, or seeking input on life's day-to-day challenges, your board can offer insights that make a real difference. And as your life evolves, your board should evolve too. Reassessing your needs and updating your board periodically ensures you'll continue to receive relevant and impactful advice. It's equally important to recognize when you might need new mentors to guide you through different stages of life or fresh challenges.

My journey with mentorship began at age seventeen, when I met one of my first advisors: a state representative (and later, a mayor). What began as a simple introduction grew into a meaningful friendship that shaped my understanding of leadership and service. That mentorship gave me the courage to run for a seat on my hometown board of education in Wausau, Wisconsin, at eighteen years old.

At the time I didn't think of mentorship strategically but was simply drawn to the wisdom and experience of people I admired. I didn't know exactly how to build these relationships or what they would involve, but I was curious about the possibilities. My connection with the legislator—and later, others—gave me the confidence to pursue public office.

That school board race became a pivotal experience. Throughout the campaign, I relied heavily on my mentors for advice and support. One of my college professors offered brutally honest yet constructive feedback, which solidified my appreciation for direct, unvarnished guidance.

The election itself was a roller coaster. On election night, early reports showed me winning, but by the next morning, the results revealed I had lost by just eighty-six votes in what was a voting constituency of about fifty-eight thousand at the time. While the outcome was disappointing, it was far from a failure. The experience introduced me to community leaders, taught me critical lessons, and gave me a lasting sense of confidence. More importantly, it reminded me that growth often comes from the journey—not just the destination.

That campaign also reinforced a fundamental truth: You don't need extraordinary credentials to build meaningful mentorships. Sometimes, all it takes is asking the right questions and seizing opportunities. My first mentoring relationship opened the door to many others. A simple question, "Who could you introduce me to that might be helpful?"—became a powerful tool for expanding my network. Much like the idea of "six degrees of separation,"[1] each introduction led to another connection.

During my first year of college, I continued building on the foundation laid by my initial advisors. I connected with the dean of students at a university meet and greet and later set up a one-on-one meeting with him to get to know him a bit more. The dean later introduced me to local leaders and helped me establish a network that profoundly shaped my future. One of my earliest "board members" was a foundation president, who introduced me to a bank CEO. That CEO, in turn, connected me with a corporate lawyer, who introduced me to a chairman overseeing

1 The six degrees of separation is the idea that all people are connected to one another through a chain of six or fewer social connections. It suggests that anyone on Earth can be linked to any other person through a small network of intermediaries. Research has been inconclusive as to the truth of this proposition. Source: Morse, Gardiner. "The Science Behind Six Degrees." HBR, February 2003. https://hbr.org/2003/02/the-science-behind-six-degrees.

multiple companies. Consequently, these relationships grew into a service-oriented network that amplified my success and reach within the community.

One meeting with the bank CEO stands out in my memory, where he reminded me that I had gained goodwill and credibility within the community for my run for office. It reminded me that I had a responsibility to make a difference where I could, which inspired me to focus my efforts on serving others and contributing to projects that benefited the greater good. By approaching my network with this mindset, I earned a seat at the table, built lasting relationships, and qualified myself to be heard when it mattered.

As my growth continued, I became increasingly intentional about building my personal board of directors. Everyone can benefit from the wisdom, experience, and ethical guidance of mentors who act as stakeholders in their lives. Imagine facing life's challenges, not alone, but with a group of skilled, objective advisors ready to help you succeed. That's the power of mentorship—and the foundation for building your board.

This book emphasizes a unique approach: building a "board of mentors" with diverse expertise and perspectives, like a corporate board of directors. This strategy recognizes the value of multiple viewpoints while highlighting the effort it takes to develop and sustain these relationships over time. While mentorship requires discipline and patience, the rewards—personal growth, clarity, and achievement—are well worth it.

Questions to journal on...

What areas of your life or career do you feel most uncertain about, and how could a mentor provide clarity or direction in those areas?

Can you identify a moment when you faced a significant challenge? How might mentorship have helped you navigate that situation?

Chapter Challenge: Research someone in your community who could be a potential mentor. Then let us know what you learned so far with the following hashtags:

Instagram, Substack and X @yourboard4life
#chapter2challenge #yourboard4life

CHAPTER 3

IDENTIFYING POTENTIAL BOARD MEMBERS

- **Who to choose—the Matrix approach:** Attracting the right mentors rather than chasing them. How diverse backgrounds matter to have varied opinions and improve problem solving.
- **Step-by-step on how to select your board:** Strategically identifying, cultivating, and communicating with a diverse group of advisors.

YOUR DECISIONS, THEIR INSIGHTS: SHAPING SUCCESS TOGETHER

When we talk about "directors," it's often in the context of the professional world. But in our context, these individuals serve as advisors or mentors in a more personal and informal sense. It's important to remember that, as the decision-maker, you retain full control over your life choices. While you might seek advice from your board of advisors, their role is to guide and support, not to decide for you. There have been times when I've taken their input into account but ultimately chosen a different path—my own "road less traveled," if you will. At the end of the day, the responsibility for your decisions rests with you.

Advisors are a bit like stakeholders in your life: They contribute their insights and expertise, but the ultimate direction is yours to determine. I've always valued independent thinking, and weighing facts objectively is a cornerstone of my decision-making process. That said, mentors are invaluable in offering new perspectives and helping you evaluate the options.

The quote, "You are the average of the five people you spend the most time with," is widely attributed to Jim Rohn, an influential motivational speaker and personal development coach. Rohn often emphasized the importance of surrounding oneself with positive influences and the impact of one's social circle on personal growth and success. I think this is an important quote to consider as you choose both your friends and mentors. Who do you want to be like?

So, what qualities should you look for when choosing your advisors? While there's no one-size-fits-all approach, here's a general framework that has worked well for me:

- **Are they exceptional in their field, community, or life?** Success can mean different things depending on the advisor's background. For example, a spiritual or community leader might be someone I admire for their impact and integrity, while a financial expert could offer deep knowledge in economics and business. It's not just about their expertise—it's about how their strengths align with what you need at a given time.
- **Do they have integrity and strong character?** Beyond expertise, integrity is crucial. I pay close attention to traits like honesty, wisdom, decency, and overall character. These qualities are essential for building trust and ensuring that their advice comes from a place of genuine care and insight.

This is where the Matrix Approach comes in (something I elaborate on below). The idea is to create a well-rounded group of advisors with diverse skills, perspectives, and experiences. This diversity ensures you're getting balanced advice, no matter the challenge. Once I've identified potential advisors based on expertise and character, I focus on cultivating relationships with them.

USING THE MATRIX FOR ADVISOR SELECTION

While my matrix may not look exactly like yours, I've found it helpful to identify specific areas where I need guidance. Each mentor brings unique strengths and perspectives, and together, they create a network of support that helps me navigate challenges and seize opportunities. Consider where you have gaps in knowledge, experience, or ability, then look for advisors in those areas.

Below, I've outlined how I've structured my matrix to guide the selection process. It's an example of how you might build your own network of mentors and advisors.

Business Lawyer

- **Role:** A skilled lawyer—particularly one specializing in business law—provides essential knowledge about protecting one's interests in contracts, negotiations, and intellectual property.
- **Mentorship Value:**
  - Offers guidance on navigating legal complexities in business.
  - Teaches negotiation tactics and strategies to achieve favorable outcomes.

    - Ensures compliance with legal regulations, minimizing risks and liabilities.

Financial Expert (Wealth Manager or Banker)

- **Role:** A financial expert helps demystify complex financial processes, such as investing, borrowing, lending, and creating sustainable business plans.
- **Mentorship Value:**
    - Educates on financial literacy and smart money management.
    - Provides insights on leveraging financial tools for growth and stability.
    - Assists in developing business plans that align with long-term goals.
    - Shares knowledge on wealth preservation and investment strategies.

Politician or Public Policy Expert

- **Role:** A mentor familiar with politics and power dynamics offers expertise in building relationships, creating coalitions, and navigating influence in professional and social arenas.
- **Mentorship Value:**
    - Guides in understanding how to build and leverage networks.
    - Offers advice on negotiating within complex power structures.

- Provides strategies for creating impactful collaborations and initiatives.
- Helps in aligning goals with broader public or organizational policies.

Educator or Academic

- **Role**: An educator or academic offers a broad perspective grounded in long-term thinking, research, and critical analysis.
- **Mentorship Value:**
  - Encourages strategic planning and visionary thinking.
  - Shares expertise across various disciplines to enrich decision-making.
  - As a decision scientist, offers frameworks for evaluating risks, benefits, and trade-offs.
  - Introduces innovative and forward-thinking approaches to challenges.

Pastor or Clergy Member

- **Role:** A pastor or clergy member provides moral and spiritual guidance, helping to ground decisions in ethical considerations and strong values.
- **Mentorship Value:**
  - Offers a "moral compass" to navigate complex personal and professional situations.
  - Helps integrate wisdom from various mentors into a cohesive, value-driven framework.

  - Provides emotional support and counseling to sustain resilience and focus.
  - Encourages reflection on deeper purposes and long-term goals.

Coach

- **Role:** A coach—whether professional, athletic, or life-focused—serves as a catalyst for growth by guiding individuals toward their goals, enhancing performance, and building endurance.
- **Mentorship Value:**
  - Helps define clear objectives and creates actionable plans to achieve them while holding the mentee accountable for progress.
  - Identifies strengths and areas for improvement, providing personalized strategies to overcome challenges and maximize effectiveness.
  - Encourages the development of emotional intelligence, effective communication, and decision-making skills to lead confidently in any context.

Mentors with Overlapping Skills

- **Role:** Many mentors possess multiple areas of expertise, which enhances their ability to provide well-rounded guidance.

- **Mentorship Value:**
    - Combines wisdom from various fields, offering holistic insights.
    - Bridges gaps between disciplines, providing innovative solutions and ideas.
    - Encourages collaboration and the cross-pollination of knowledge.

Together, these experts form a dynamic and well-rounded board of directors capable of addressing a wide array of challenges and opportunities. These were the ones I chose; you may have a different group of mentors in mind. Perhaps you need artistic rather than political advice, so you would select creative types. Or perhaps you are into technology—you would then be seeking out an engineer or entrepreneur in this space.

The attributes I admired most in my mentors were integrity, discipline, intelligence, and independent thinking. While independent thinking was important, I didn't always require it. In fact, conventional thinking often provided a helpful foundation, allowing me to weigh diverse perspectives. I believe there's immense value in traditional approaches, as they've stood the test of time. As much as I consider myself a contrarian, it's not for the sake of being contrary but to exercise critical thinking. After analyzing an issue, I adopt whatever approach—conventional or unconventional—makes the most sense. A profoundly disheartening modern phenomenon is the seemingly increasing rarity (or decreasing practice) of critical thinking, as it is no longer emphasized in education.

FROM COURT TO CHARACTER: STEPH CURRY'S JOURNEY WITH A LIFE BOARD OF MENTORS

Steph Curry's journey to becoming one of the greatest basketball players of all time is a story deeply intertwined with mentorship, guidance, and an evolving Board of Directors for Life.

From a young age, Steph's first and most influential mentor was his father, **Dell Curry.** As a former NBA player, Dell didn't just teach Steph the mechanics of shooting a basketball; he instilled in him a relentless work ethic and a deep appreciation for the game. Steph often recounts the hours spent watching his father play and practicing alongside him, soaking in not just skills, but life lessons about humility, professionalism, and perseverance. Alongside Dell was **Sonya Curry,** Steph's mother, who added another layer of mentorship. Sonya emphasized discipline and the importance of education, faith, and accountability. Together, they built a foundation of character that would sustain Steph through the highs and lows of his career.

As Steph stepped into his own path, other mentors emerged. At Davidson College, **Coach Bob McKillop** played a transformative role. Where others saw an undersized player with limited potential, McKillop saw greatness. He nurtured Steph's confidence, teaching him to lead not just by his skills but by his presence and determination. Under McKillop's guidance, Steph evolved into a leader who could inspire his team through both words and actions.

When Steph entered the NBA, mentorship continued to shape his path. Early in his career, then–Golden State Warriors coach **Mark Jackson** encouraged him to embrace his unique gifts and play with confidence. Jackson's vision for the Warriors as a team built around shooting, and teamwork allowed Steph to thrive and revolutionize the game of basketball.

Beyond traditional mentors, Steph found inspiration and support in his peers. Teammates like **Andre Iguodala, Klay Thompson,** and **Draymond Green** acted as a support system, pushing him to grow both as a player and a leader. Iguodala, as a veteran, modeled professionalism and poise, while Thompson and Green fostered a culture of accountability and camaraderie that brought out the best in Steph.

Off the court, Steph leaned on spiritual mentors and faith leaders who helped him maintain perspective and gratitude. His Christian faith has been a guiding force in his life, shaping how he approaches success, failure, and everything in between. Life coaches and advisors have also played their part, helping Steph navigate the challenges of fame and personal growth.

Looking at Steph Curry's life, it becomes clear that he developed his own board. Much like a corporate board guides an organization, this diverse group of mentors, family members, peers, and advisors has guided Steph in different facets of his life—both on and off the court. Each person brought unique strengths: Dell Curry provided expertise and wisdom in basketball, Sonya Curry emphasized discipline and character, Bob McKillop cultivated leadership, and teammates like Iguodala and Green offered peer accountability. Spiritual mentors and faith leaders kept him grounded, while coaches like Mark Jackson inspired confidence in his revolutionary style of play.

This "board" wasn't built intentionally, but its influence has been profound. It highlights how surrounding yourself with people who challenge, support, and guide you can transform potential into achievement. For Steph Curry, it wasn't just about basketball; it was about becoming a whole person, shaped by the collective wisdom and care of those around him. His story is a testament to the power of mentorship and the value of building a network of advisors who believe in you—sometimes even more than you believe in yourself.

PARENTS: THE ORIGINAL MEMBERS OF YOUR SUPPORT BOARD

I must acknowledge my parents' pivotal role in shaping me and my development. **My mother** was an exceptional problem solver with resilience and determination equivalent to a small army. She was fearless and unyielding, sometimes to an extreme, but this trait, when tempered, became a quality I embraced. It taught me to stand up for what I believed.

It started out early. I recall an incident in second grade when a classmate bullied me relentlessly. I asked my teacher to move my desk away from the bully, but she refused. My mother advised me to stand my ground, telling me to let the teacher know that if she didn't move me, I wouldn't cooperate in class any further. While I expected my mother to intervene directly, she insisted I handle it myself. The next day, I stood before the class and told the teacher I wouldn't relent until she addressed the issue. Surprised, the teacher promptly moved me, and the bullying stopped (well, for a bit). That experience taught me to stand up for what was right, knowing my parents would always support me. But even if they didn't, I had to learn to stand up for myself. I later stood up to the bully, and we became friends after that.

My mother was also a deeply spiritual person, instilling in me a robust set of values through her faith in God. She was extraordinarily generous, often to a fault, so when she was awarded a financial settlement from losing her hand in an accident a few years before I was born, she ended up giving away much of her money. As a result of her generosity, in her later years I had to help support her financially, but I believe it's far better to be overly generous than not generous enough. My motto when it comes to generosity is that *you can always afford to be generous, but you can't always afford not to be.* This sounds oxymoronic, but I believe I can always afford to be generous because generosity doesn't have to mean giving away significant resources—it can be as simple as offering my time, kindness, attention, or support. No matter my circumstances, there's always a meaningful way to give.

I also understand that not being generous can have consequences. By holding back, I might lose valuable opportunities to earn trust, strengthen connections, or develop as an individual. The costs of selfishness—like strained relationships, lost goodwill, or regret—often outweigh the effort it takes to be generous. For me, generosity is a practice that enriches my life and the lives of others, no matter what I have to give. (I recommend the book *The Psychology of Money* by Morgan Housel, which touches on this well.)

My father was an equally remarkable role model. A World War II submariner in the South Pacific, he was disciplined, hardworking, and unwavering in his principles. He had me late in life (he was in his late forties) as the youngest of five—a "surprise baby." He was a man of few words, but when he spoke, it was meaningful. His reliability and integrity were constants in my childhood. I knew that if he promised something, I could count on it without question. He refrained from vices like drinking, smoking, or swearing and was wholly dedicated to his work and providing for his family. From him, I learned the importance of discipline, hard work, and being a person of your word.

My parents imparted invaluable lessons in moral fortitude, determination, and independence. These qualities have shaped my approach to mentorship, allowing me to build meaningful relationships while maintaining independence. I've learned to respectfully submit to more experienced authorities, fostering discipline, patience, and trust. My mentors and the foundational values my parents instilled have been instrumental in my personal and professional growth.

FROM QUESTIONS TO CHEMISTRY: LET MENTORSHIP EVOLVE NATURALLY

When I was in college and reaching out to potential advisors, I always made sure my approach was professional. I'd set up an appointment through a formal introduction and ensure I was on time—punctuality is key. If possible, always meet in person. Avoid virtual meetings! It's just too impersonal, and you miss out on picking up on subtle forms of communication that are critical to reading people. If meeting in person isn't an option, meeting virtually is fine, but do what you can to make that first connection face-to-face. Follow-up meetings online? Totally fine.

When you do meet a potential mentor, come prepared. Dress professionally, and have an agenda, specific questions, and a clear purpose for the meeting. The questions I typically ask are about their personal experiences—how they got to where they are, the advice they received when they were my age, and what values guide their decisions. These questions are the foundation of any good mentor-mentee relationship because you'll always be learning from your advisors. One tip: steer clear of controversial topics like religion or politics unless your relationship is specifically built around those areas. Divisive topics don't always help you get to know someone better. I've had mentors on the opposite side of the political aisle, and I loved having them as advisors because they challenged my perspective in the best ways.

When reaching out, it's also important to demonstrate your potential and what makes you stand out. Now, this doesn't mean overselling yourself, but it does mean presenting yourself as someone worth investing time in. Exceptional people—those you're seeking as mentors—love giving back and contributing, but they're discerning about where to focus their time. Show that you're exceptional, driven, and eager to learn. Time is their most valuable commodity, so prove that you won't waste it.

Pay close attention to the flow of the conversation. Follow the mentor's lead—if they're interested in continuing the conversation, they'll usually let you know. Don't push it. And here's what *not* to do: Don't ask outright, "Will you be my mentor/advisor?" That can feel like a huge commitment for someone who's just met you. In fact, I would almost never ask this question. Instead, let the relationship evolve naturally over time. It's way less awkward and works much better. This approach has served me well.

Now, not every meeting will be a home run. Sometimes you'll meet someone and realize they're not a good fit as an advisor, or they might outright say they're not interested. Maybe the chemistry just isn't there. That's okay—move on! It wasn't meant to be. Keep making an effort, and you'll eventually find the right people. Sometimes, yes, you have to "kiss a lot of frogs" before you find your prince or princess.

FORTUNE FAVORS THE PREPARED

So let's review how to approach your potential mentors/advisors:

Approach Potential Advisors Professionally

- Be introduced when possible and set an appointment in advance.
- Always arrive on time and meet in person whenever possible to establish a personal connection and improve communication skills.
- If meeting in person is impossible, schedule a virtual meeting. But again, start with an in-person meeting whenever feasible, then follow up with virtual meetings as needed.

Prepare for the Meeting

- Research the prospective mentor's professional and academic background, achievements, and affiliations.
- Dress professionally to make a positive impression.
- Come with an agenda, specific questions, and a clear ask to demonstrate preparation and respect for their time.

Ask Insightful Questions

- Focus on their personal experiences, such as how they achieved success, the advice they valued at your age, and what they prioritize most.
- Avoid divisive or controversial topics like religion or politics unless these are central to the relationship's context.

Foster Mutual Respect

- Understand and value people beyond labels, appreciating the depth of their experiences and perspectives, even if they differ from your own.

Demonstrate Your Potential

- Highlight your exceptional qualities and initiative without overselling yourself.
- Show that you are worth their time by displaying professionalism, potential, and a willingness to learn.

Be Sensitive to the Flow of the Conversation

- Let the advisor guide the discussion and take cues from their interest and willingness to continue the relationship.
- Avoid directly asking, "Will you be my mentor/advisor?" as it may feel like too much of a commitment up front.

Accept Outcomes Gracefully

- Recognize that not every interaction will result in a mentor relationship.
- If the person isn't a good fit or the relationship doesn't progress, take it as a learning experience and move on professionally.

STEP-BY-STEP: HOW TO BUILD YOUR BOARD OF ADVISORS

When selecting your advisors, here are some steps to consider. Though the following aren't necessarily in order of importance, it's the approach I usually take.

Define Your Needs and Goals

- Step: Understand what areas of your life or career need guidance, meaning one must "know thyself." Consider your professional and personal goals and which fields or sectors are essential for your development.
- Example: If you are starting a business, you might want advisors who can help with finance, marketing, legal issues, and networking.
- Why This Matters: It helps narrow down the types of individuals you should approach. You need to know what specific expertise will help you achieve your objectives.

Identify Potential Advisors in Your Network

- Step: Look for people in your existing network first who demonstrate the qualities you admire. This could include colleagues, family, friends, or people you've encountered through work or volunteering.
- Example: A mentor could be a former professor, a manager interested in your development, or a professional you've worked with at a nonprofit organization.

- Why This Matters: Your existing network is often the best place to start. These people already know you and are more likely to be receptive.

Expand Beyond Your Network

- Step: If your network doesn't contain the right people, or if your needs evolve and you've utilized everyone in your network, you may need to ask for introductions to persons who fit your new criteria. You may also need to attend conferences, join professional groups, or participate in community events to meet potential mentors.
- Example: Ask an existing contact or connection, perhaps a teacher or coach, who they could introduce you to that would advance your goals. You can also attend industry-specific events or volunteer for causes where influential people might be involved. Networking at these events allows you to meet people you wouldn't otherwise encounter. If you're in school, often that environment has lots of opportunities to meet people and make connections. Universities are catalysts for influencers and decision-makers in a myriad of professions. Social media—including LinkedIn, Facebook, and Instagram—and other tools are excellent at helping you find and connect with others as well.
- Why This Matters: Sometimes your initial network won't be enough to support all your goals, and expanding your horizons is necessary to access your expertise.

Evaluate Their Expertise and Character

- Step: Before approaching someone to be on your board of directors, research their achievements, reputation, and integrity. You're looking for people who have the proper knowledge and demonstrate strong values, honesty, and leadership.
- Example: If you admire someone's leadership style or how they're regarded in their industry or community, that person may be a good candidate. Consider personality attributes as well if you can.
- Why This Matters: It's not just about what they know—it's also about who they are. You want advisors with both expertise and strong character that you click with as well.

Reach Out with a Clear Ask

- Step: When you first approach someone, make your intentions clear. Let them know you admire their work and would appreciate their guidance in specific areas. Don't ask them to formally join your "board of advisors"; this is a relationship that will build with time.
- Example: "Your community work inspires me, and I would love to learn more about how you built your career. Could I ask you for advice on how to grow in my field?"
- Why This Matters: An explicit, direct request shows respect for their time and demonstrates your seriousness. Keep the initial proposal small—a

conversation or coffee meeting to start—and then build from there.

Build Genuine Relationships

- Step: Establish a relationship based on mutual respect. *Be authentic.* Offer your help if needed and always show appreciation for their time and advice.
- Example: After you receive advice, follow up and let them know how it impacted your decision or progress. Offer to support them by attending their events or volunteering your time.
- Why This Matters: Mentorship is a two-way street. Offering value in return and maintaining consistent communication deepens the relationship.

Diversify Your Advisory Board (Create a Matrix)

- Step: Ensure you have advisors from different fields and with varying expertise. This matrix should include professionals from industries you want to enter, community leaders, and even people with spiritual or personal insight. Take the time and use Myers-Briggs to understand where your personality fits with theirs. (More on Myers-Briggs in the next chapter.)
- Example: Your board could include a financial expert, a lawyer, a business leader, a philanthropist, and a spiritual or religious advisor. Each one guides you in different areas of your life.

- Why This Matters: A diverse board of advisors brings well-rounded perspectives, ensuring you have access to varied knowledge, skills, and viewpoints.

Be Grateful and Keep in Touch

- Step: Regularly check in with your advisors. Keep them updated on your progress and appreciate their role in your development.
- Example: Send thank-you notes, provide updates on how their advice has helped you, and find ways to show your gratitude over time.
- Why This Matters: Gratitude reinforces the relationship and demonstrates that you value their input. It also encourages them to continue investing in your success. After your first meeting, be sure to follow up with a thank-you note or email. Thank them for their time and acknowledge something they said in conversation to show that you were listening and synthesizing the information they shared with you.

YOU DON'T HAVE TO BE CONNECTED TO GET CONNECTED

One of the best ways to start is by looking at who you already know in your network. Some of them could be potential advisors, or they may introduce you to someone who might be. When I started at seventeen, I didn't have any network. My parents weren't social or well-connected in the community where we lived. My mom was a stay-at-home parent who focused all her time on caring for us kids. She only had a small group of friends. My dad worked in construction as a subcontractor, traveling nationwide for projects. He barely knew anyone outside his work and almost no one in our community.

Don't think you need a well-connected family or influential relatives to start building your network. When I first became interested in politics, I didn't know anyone in the field, so I volunteered for a local politician's campaign. Later, as a college freshman, I reached out to the dean to share some project ideas I wanted to pursue. He appreciated my initiative and introduced me to a foundation president who ended up donating to the project I was working on. From there, I started building relationships with significant community leaders and influencers—all within less than a year. It all started with taking the first step.

The first time I met my bank CEO mentor, he surprised me by saying he already knew who I was—he had voted for me during my run for school board! That experience gave me some credibility and social equity in the community, which helped open doors.

But today, young people have a big advantage I didn't have back then: social media. Platforms like LinkedIn, Instagram, and Facebook make it easier than ever to connect with people you admire.

Here's a tip: Use social media to see who in your network knows someone you'd like to meet and ask if they'd be willing to introduce you.

A warm introduction always works better than cold calling or sending a random email. Beyond social media, reach out to family, friends, or colleagues and ask if they know anyone who could serve as a great mentor or advisor. It might take some research and patience to identify the right people and figure out the best way to connect, but don't give up. Even if someone seems famous or out of reach, it's worth trying. You never know until you ask.

In fact, I just recently reached out via Instagram to an author I really liked, and we started to talk via Messenger, then did a Zoom call (as he was not in the United States), and now we have arranged to meet up when he's in the U.S. for a book tour. It's so much easier to meet people now than when I first started out.

Whenever you get the opportunity to connect with someone, look for ways to stand out. Whether it's through achievements in sports, academics, or the arts, whatever makes you unique and exceptional, highlight those when introducing yourself or requesting a meeting. It shows ambition and potential, which men-

Your Talents Are the Key to New Connections

A recent example that comes to mind is a college student named Daniel, whom I recently met while speaking on mentorship at a college. He shared how he had been learning from influencers and businesspeople he met while working as a caddie at a golf course in a small town in Ohio. Daniel was already beginning to build mentorships without realizing it—he just needed to take the next step.

Daniel combined his love for golf and his natural talent to secure a job as a caddie, which brought him into contact with successful leaders in his community from the local country club. While serving them on the course, he listened to their discussions on business, politics, and various other topics, learning all along the way. He was also building relationships with these people.

It didn't matter whether he was from a small town or just a teenager, nor did his socioeconomic situation matter. What mattered was that he had something to offer—his skills as a caddie and golfer—and he was in the right place at the right time, fulfilling a need.

Now that Daniel has begun forming these connections on the golf course, he can meet them outside of work, perhaps over coffee or lunch, to discuss mutual interests and further develop those mentorship and advisor relationships.

Everyone has talents or interests, and those can be leveraged to connect with people. Daniel's story is remarkable because he has connected with a diverse group of professionals, all united by their love of golf, giving him access to a strong pool of potential advisors/mentors. He didn't have to chase these mentors; they came to him.

tors appreciate. That said, none of this works if you don't believe in yourself. Confidence in your abilities and potential is key. So, take a deep breath, trust in what you bring to the table, and go for it!

THE POWER OF PLACE

As I continued progressing through school and into my career, I was introduced to more and more people—often because I asked for those introductions. I had transferred to Westmont College in Santa Barbara, California, and by the time I graduated, I had built strong connections in politics, business, entertainment, and education. These relationships eventually formed my Board of Directors for Life, a group of trusted advisors I've maintained for over twenty years.

Creating a board like this goes beyond simply finding people who can give good advice. It's about building meaningful, lasting relationships with individuals who inspire, guide, and challenge you—while also finding ways to offer value to them in return. Your advisory network can become one of your greatest resources, but ultimately, your success depends on you. Be intentional about choosing, building, and nurturing these relationships. It's one of the best investments you can make for your future.

As I began my career in Santa Barbara, friends and professional acquaintances often told me that I should move to a bigger city like Los Angeles, New York, or London, where there were more opportunities. I didn't agree with this assessment. I chose Santa Barbara because it was a small town with big fish in it (small pond, big fish: I assume everyone reading this understands the reference).

Santa Barbara is home to some of the most successful people in the world from media, tech, entertainment, and other industries. While they may work in Los Angeles or elsewhere, they live in Santa Barbara, serve on boards locally, send their children to school there, and participate in community events. They are more relaxed, more approachable, and the opportunities to work with them are far greater in a community of about one hundred thousand than in a community of five million or more.

In Los Angeles, New York, London, and similar cities, I would have been competing with thousands of other up-and-coming professionals—not only to get attention but also to prove myself in a professional role. In Santa Barbara, I was competing with maybe a hundred, probably far fewer. Once I established working relationships with some of these "big fish," the rest of the world became available to me professionally. I sidestepped the competition and worked on meaningful projects with high-level influencers much earlier in my career.

This was no accident; it was part of a strategy I had decided on even before transferring to Santa Barbara to finish college. Starting out in a small town can have its benefits, especially if it's the right town.

Questions to journal on...

What qualities or characteristics are most important to you in a mentor, and how do these align with your current goals?

Who in your current network inspires you, and how could they contribute to your personal board of directors?

Chapter Challenge: Who is someone you consider a mentor? List the qualities that you most admire.

Instagram, Substack and X @yourboard4life
#chapter3challenge #yourboard4life

CHAPTER 4

THE POWER OF DIVERSE PERSPECTIVES

- **Having a diverse board of directors (a matrix):** People from different backgrounds, industries, and life experiences. Diverse perspectives lead to more balanced decision-making and greater innovation.
- **Setting goals:** Identify personal and professional goals, which will guide you in selecting the right mentors.
- **Personality and fit:** Use Myers-Briggs to tailor mentorship to personality strengths and communication styles.

BROADER PERSPECTIVES, BETTER DECISIONS

One of the key ideas in this book is the importance of having multiple mentors from diverse backgrounds instead of relying on just one person. The idea is simple: When you have a variety of advisors, each brings their own unique perspective and expertise, giving you a more well-rounded view. Seeking advice from multiple sources isn't a sign of indecision—it's actually a sign of strength and wisdom.

For example, imagine you're an entrepreneur launching a new business. If you only sought advice from a successful entrepreneur in your field, you'd gain valuable insights specific to your industry. But what about legal challenges, marketing strategies, leadership styles, or even maintaining your health and endurance? By connecting with a lawyer, a marketing expert, a leadership coach, and a trainer, you can see the bigger picture and prepare for both the challenges and opportunities ahead. Each person's guidance adds depth to your decisions and helps you approach your goals more confidently.

I'd start with a matrix to help me categorize my needs and potential mentors. Here's just an example:

Mentor	Professional Expertise	Role/Contribution
Advisor 1: Finance	CPA/banker/ wealth manager	Provide advice on financial matters
Advisor 2: Niche Profession	Person in your professional circle	Provide career-specific knowledge/experience
Advisor 3: Spiritual or Relational	A clergy member/therapist	Provide emotional/ spiritual advice
Advisor 4: Leadership	Community leader/expert	Provide advice on decision-making/ leadership
Advisor 5: Leadership/ Diverse Fields	Leader/expert in diverse field	Provide advice on strategic moves/ decision-making/health
Advisor 6: Legal	An attorney or legal advisor	Provide advice on legal matters

The idea of creating a matrix is to help you identify the areas of expertise or traits you need represented in your personal advisory board and define the roles or types of advisors who can fill those needs. It's a way to think intentionally about the support you need and how to build a network that aligns with your goals. It also shows you where you may have "gaps" in your knowledge or skill base and can help you fill those in.

To explain this concept, let's borrow an example from nonprofit boards. While a nonprofit is an organization and not an individual, the principles still apply. Nonprofit boards often focus on three key contributions from their board members: time, talent, and treasure. Though not the same categories for individuals, I think you can see the idea I'm trying to convey using this example.

- **Time** refers to individuals who can dedicate energy and effort to support the organization's cause or operational needs.
- **Talent** includes people with specific expertise—like legal, financial, or marketing skills—who can offer valuable advice or technical support.
- **Treasure** involves those who can either contribute financially or use their networks to secure resources.

This framework can also work when thinking about your personal advisory matrix. What areas of your life or career need the most guidance? Maybe you're looking for emotional support to handle challenges, financial advice to manage resources, legal expertise for a specific situation, or career mentorship to help you grow professionally. In most cases, you'll need a mix of these. By identifying the specific skill sets or types of guidance you need and finding individuals who align with those areas, you can build a well-rounded board to help you achieve your goals.

Approaching this with clarity and intention ensures that your advisory network aligns with your aspirations for life and work. Having diverse perspectives on your board can be a game-changer. Sometimes, when we're focused on a specific goal, it's easy to overlook alternative paths or potential challenges, and we get tunnel vision. Consulting with a range of people can highlight blind spots and make your plans stronger and more resilient. Remember, no matter your age, career stage, or level of success, there's always something to gain from external viewpoints.

In my own experience, I started with a circle of advisors who were mostly men. Progressively, I realized I was missing out on valuable insights by not including women in my network. That realization prompted me to seek out relationships with female mentors. For example, I connected with a female professor who became a significant influence, and later, I developed relationships with a multi-Emmy-Award-winning actress as well as a one-time *New York Times* journalist and author. These women provided perspectives that complemented what I was already hearing from my male mentors, giving me a broader and more balanced understanding of personal and professional challenges.

FROM RUNWAY TO BOARDROOM: KATHY IRELAND'S BLUEPRINT FOR RESILIENT SUCCESS

Kathy Ireland's rise to fame as a supermodel was nothing short of dazzling. In the 1980s and 1990s, she graced the cover of *Sports Illustrated* three times, including its best-selling swimsuit issue of all time. But Ireland knew something most models at the peak of their careers often overlooked—modeling had a shelf life, and she needed to build something that would last beyond the runway.

What many didn't see beneath the glamorous exterior was a woman with sharp business instincts and an unwavering drive. She wasn't interested in being just another celebrity-endorsed brand; she wanted to create something real, sustainable, and impactful. And she wasn't going to do it alone.

Supermodel to Businesswoman

In 1993, Ireland launched what many considered an unlikely business venture—a line of socks sold through Kmart. The fashion world dismissed it, but she saw an opportunity to serve "real people with real needs." It wasn't about glamour—it was about practicality and accessibility. That simple sock line became the foundation of what would later grow into a $2 billion global empire.

By 1999, she had set her sights on a new industry—home furnishings. It was then that **Warren Buffett,** one of the world's most revered investors, entered the picture. Partnering with Buffett's Nebraska Furniture Mart, a subsidiary of Berkshire Hathaway, Ireland gained invaluable insight into the power of long-term investment and market stability. Buffett's advice was clear: focus on industries that endure, not fleeting trends. Ireland took that wisdom to heart, building a brand that now spans furniture, fashion, beauty, pet care, and education.

Weathering the Storms of Business

Success wasn't without its challenges. The 9/11 attacks devastated the retail industry, forcing Ireland to rethink her business strategy. Just a year later, Kmart's bankruptcy threatened to pull the rug out from under her. But instead of retreating, she diversified her retail partnerships, ensuring that no single company could dictate her success.

Then came the COVID-19 pandemic—a crisis that hit close to home. Her husband, Gregory, an emergency room physician, contracted the virus, as did Stephen Roseberry, the president of Kathy

Ireland Worldwide (kiWW). Suddenly, health and safety weren't just priorities for her business; they became personal battles.

Fortunately, Roseberry's foresight to decentralize the company years earlier meant kiWW could pivot quickly. By embracing remote work and digital tools, Ireland's team remained seamlessly connected. Through it all, she held on to one core belief: Change is inevitable—either you take control of it, or it takes control of you.

Wisdom from Elizabeth Taylor

One of Ireland's most cherished mentors was **Elizabeth Taylor.** Known for her legendary acting career and humanitarian work, Taylor taught Ireland one of the most important lessons of her life—align business with values.

Taylor's fearless advocacy for HIV/AIDS awareness showed Ireland the power of using success for a greater good. Inspired by her mentor, Ireland made philanthropy a cornerstone of her company. Today, kiWW supports education, health care, and social causes, embodying Taylor's belief that true success isn't measured by wealth but by impact.

The Power of a Board of Directors for Life

Ireland didn't just rely on one or two mentors—she built a network of trusted advisors whom she called her "board of advisors." Among them was her mother, **Barbara,** who played an early and profound role in shaping her resilience and faith.

Before Ireland set off on her first modeling trip, her mother placed a Bible in her suitcase. It became a guiding force throughout her life. Barbara's advice was simple yet profound: "If you've prayed about something and don't have peace, it's not God's will."

That wisdom shaped how Ireland made decisions, both personally and professionally.

Her relationship with Warren Buffett is another example of mentorship that has stood the test of time. She regularly attends Berkshire Hathaway's shareholder meetings, even competing against Buffett in his famous newspaper toss—a lighthearted nod to their shared childhood experience as paper carriers.

Lessons in Trust, Change, and Resilience

While Ireland believes in long-term relationships, she also understands that not every connection is meant to last forever. Experience taught her that trust must be earned, and sometimes, even strong relationships must evolve—or end.

Still, she emphasizes that mentorship is one of the most valuable tools for success. The key is to surround yourself with people who challenge you, hold you accountable, and genuinely want to see you succeed.

A Legacy of Impact

Today, Kathy Ireland Worldwide stands as one of the most admired global brands, consistently ranked alongside Martha Stewart and Ralph Lauren. But for Ireland, success isn't just about business—it's about making a difference.

Her journey from runway to boardroom is proof that mentorship, adaptability, and resilience can transform obstacles into stepping stones. She embraced guidance, navigated setbacks, and built a business rooted in integrity.

And at the core of it all? A simple but powerful philosophy: Surround yourself with people who make you better, stay true to your values, and never be afraid to pivot when life demands it.

Her story isn't just about success—it's about building a life of purpose and impact.

UNEXPECTED VOICES, UNPARALLELED INSIGHTS

Intentionally building a diverse advisory board takes effort, but the rewards are worth it. It's an investment in your growth, resilience, and success.

Diversity isn't just about gender, ethnicity, or professional background—it also includes life experiences. Some of my most impactful mentors weren't the traditionally "successful" or high-status individuals you might expect. Instead, they were people who had faced challenges, gained hard-earned wisdom, and offered unique perspectives that more conventional mentors simply couldn't.

One of my most meaningful mentors was a steady, humble individual who didn't hold a prestigious title or high-profile position. What they did offer was a grounded, practical outlook and a depth of wisdom that only comes from life experience. Their guidance was emotionally and spiritually uplifting, and they helped me see myself in a new light—something that allowed me to redefine my own path.

This relationship lasted only about a year or two, but it came at a time when I was going through significant struggles. This mentor turned out to be exactly the right person at the right moment. Though life eventually took us in different directions, I remain deeply grateful for the role they played during that time. Not every mentorship is long-term, and that's okay. Some connections are meant to be short-term, offering just what you need at a specific point in your life.

Being open to learning from a wide range of people can lead to unexpected growth. Often, it's the individuals who don't perfectly align with your beliefs—whether politically, religiously, or otherwise—who can offer some of the most valuable advice. By remaining open, you create opportunities to gain insights and perspectives that might not come from more traditional sources.

GOALS WITH GUIDANCE: UNLOCKING SUCCESS THROUGH DIVERSE MENTORSHIP

Setting goals is a cornerstone of both personal and professional development. To truly benefit from mentorship, your chosen advisors should align with your aspirations while also challenging you to think in new and diverse ways. While many of your mentors may have already achieved the things you hope to accomplish, don't overlook those who might bring an unconventional perspective. Often, the most unexpected mentors offer insights or support in areas you didn't even realize you needed.

For example, one of my long-term goals has been to build a diverse network of professionals from various industries to support my entrepreneurial journey and my interest in running for office someday. To achieve this, I sought out mentors from fields as varied as business, entertainment, and academia. Each mentor had a distinct approach to networking and success, and their collective wisdom helped me refine my strategies. While some offered specialized, industry-specific advice, others shared broader life lessons about integrity, resilience, and effective communication—skills that are invaluable in any field.

For young people in their twenties, it's natural to feel confident in their perspectives and embrace a modern, independent outlook on life. This is often a time of self-discovery and exploration, filled with opportunities to define your identity and carve your own path. Yet it can also be incredibly enriching to seek out guidance from mentors, teachers, or even parents who have walked similar paths before you. Their insights can offer a broader perspective, helping you navigate challenges with greater clarity and confidence.

While every generation faces its own unique technological and social changes, the fundamentals of human relationships, decision-making, and personal growth remain consistent. The wisdom of older mentors—who have weathered the ups and downs of life—can help you see patterns and trends more clearly. They've often experienced the rise and fall of ideas and can guide you through decisions with the benefit of hindsight.

For instance, one of my most formative mentorships was with a university dean. What began as an exchange of ideas soon evolved into a key advisory relationship. He became a guiding force as I dove into campus projects, offering encouragement and turning our regular meetings into a true partnership. Beyond advice, he connected me to influential community leaders, including a foundation president who later introduced me to a bank CEO, a lawyer, and a corporate chairman—individuals I've mentioned earlier in this book.

By the time I was twenty, I was collaborating with these high-level professionals on various projects. These experiences not only helped me build meaningful relationships but also allowed me to learn from their expertise and observe their character.

PERSONALITY: FINDING THE RIGHT FIT

Understanding the personalities and values of these individuals was an informal process at first, but over time, I realized how valuable it was to approach this intentionally. A more formal understanding of mentorship and relationship-building deepened my ability to connect with and learn from these remarkable individuals.

Collaboration is a balance of give and take, and understanding how your personality interacts with others—and vice versa—is both valuable and worth exploring. There are many tools you can use to do this, and one tool I have found helpful is the Myers-Briggs personality assessment. I'm an introvert, and I mention this because many people assume that my ability to connect with others and navigate the complexities of mentor-mentee relationships comes naturally, so I must be an extrovert. But that's not the case. I had to *learn* to be extroverted. I had to challenge myself to step out of my comfort zone and into socially uncomfortable situations in order to grow.

If you are an introvert, let this be an encouragement to you: *You can do this too.* Don't use your introverted nature as an excuse to avoid putting yourself out there. Yes, it might feel awkward at times, but that discomfort is where growth happens. If you let introversion become an excuse, you're only cheating yourself out of incredible experiences and meaningful relationships. And at the end of the day, those connections—however uncomfortable they may seem at first—are what truly help you learn and grow.

I am including this explanation of Myers-Briggs and how to use the tools it provides to help you in identifying and working with various personalities and, therefore, finding good mentors.

When viewed through the Myers-Briggs Type Indicator (MBTI), mentorship can provide valuable insights into selecting the right mentors to support personal and professional growth. The MBTI categorizes individuals into sixteen personality types based on their preferences in four dimensions: Extraversion vs.

Introversion, Sensing vs. Intuitive, Thinking vs. Feeling, and Judging vs. Perceiving. Understanding these preferences can help mentees identify mentors who complement their strengths, challenge their blind spots, and align with their learning styles.

For example, if you are an Introvert (I), you might benefit from a mentor who is more outgoing and socially dynamic, or an Extravert (E). Such a mentor could encourage you to step out of your comfort zone, expand your network, and navigate social interactions more effectively. On the other hand, if you're an Extravert, an Introverted mentor could help you develop reflective thinking and foster a more thoughtful approach to decision-making.

Similarly, the Sensing (S) vs. Intuition (N) dimension can guide the selection of a mentor who aligns with your preferred way of processing information. A Sensing mentor who focuses on concrete details and practical advice could benefit someone with Intuitive inclinations by grounding their visionary ideas in actionable steps. Conversely, an Intuitive mentor could inspire a Sensing individual to think beyond immediate realities and explore long-term possibilities.

The Thinking (T) vs. Feeling (F) dimension highlights differences in decision-making. A Thinking mentor, who emphasizes logic and objectivity, may be ideal for someone looking to develop analytical and strategic skills. Alternatively, a Feeling mentor could help a Thinking mentee navigate interpersonal relationships and lead with empathy and emotional intelligence.

Finally, the Judging (J) vs. Perceiving (P) preference can shape mentorship dynamics. A Judging mentor, who values structure and planning, might provide clarity and organization to a Perceiving mentee, who thrives in flexibility but struggles with follow-through. Conversely, a Perceiving mentor could teach a

Judging mentee to embrace adaptability and open-mindedness in a world of constant change.

By considering your own MBTI type and the type of mentor who complements or challenges your preferences, you can build a mentorship relationship that is both balanced and enriching. This intentional alignment ensures that your mentor supports your strengths and helps you grow in areas where you may need development, creating a truly transformative experience.

Learning your personality type is easy. There are books and online resources, some of which are free, that can test you and help you determine your type. Figuring out what type of mentor someone might be isn't always obvious—it's something you often discover over time as you get to know them, their background, and their personality. As you build that relationship, you might eventually feel comfortable asking if they're familiar with the Myers-Briggs personality types and whether they know their own. If they don't, you can always suggest they investigate it. It's not just helpful for you—it can also give them valuable insight into their own interpersonal communication style.

Questions to journal on...

What unique perspectives or experiences do you currently lack in your network, and how could including mentors from diverse backgrounds enhance your decision-making and creativity?

How can you ensure that your personal board of directors reflects a variety of industries, cultures, or experiences to help you approach challenges from multiple perspectives?

Chapter Challenge: What steps can you take to actively seek out mentors who might challenge your thinking or provide insights outside your usual frame of reference?

Instagram, Substack and X @yourboard4life
#chapter4challenge #yourboard4life

CHAPTER 5

BUILDING AND NURTURING BOARD RELATIONSHIPS

- **Relationship building:** Strategies for developing and maintaining strong relationships with advisors. The importance of mutual respect, regular communication, and appreciation for the mentor's time and guidance.
- **Authenticity matters:** Being authentic is your key to sound connections.
- **Journey or dance?** Learn to be present with Alan Watts.

BUILDING BONDS, NOT JUST NETWORKS: THE HEART OF MENTORSHIP

Again, building a board of mentors is about more than just seeking guidance—it's about creating meaningful, long-lasting relationships. The individuals you choose as advisors become important stakeholders in your journey, and maintaining these relationships requires thoughtfulness, communication, and mutual respect. It's not a one-way street; mentorship thrives on reciprocity, clear boundaries, and active engagement from both sides. As JFK once said, "Ask not what your mentor can do for you but what you can do for your mentor..." or something like that (with a little of my own creative license).

Nurturing these relationships also means being mindful of boundaries. While it might be tempting to consult with your mentors about every challenge or idea, respecting their time is crucial. Balancing how often you seek their involvement helps sustain the relationship in the long run. When reaching out, approach them with well-thought-out, meaningful questions rather than frequent, smaller inquiries. Demonstrating that you value their time and expertise shows respect and makes them more likely to invest in your growth. Thoughtful communication, paired with initiative and commitment, builds trust and fosters a relationship where both parties feel they are contributing something valuable. It also encourages you to develop problem-solving skills on your own—an essential step for future independence.

COMMUNICATION AND BOUNDARIES

Effective communication is key to maintaining and growing your mentor relationships. It's all about finding the right balance—keeping your mentors engaged without overwhelming them. One of the benefits of having multiple mentors is the ability to approach different people for specific issues. For smaller, more frequent questions, you might go to a mentor you're most comfortable with. For bigger, strategic decisions, it may be better to consult the group as a whole. By spreading out your requests, you avoid overburdening any one person and get to benefit from the unique strengths of each mentor.

It's also important to remember that communication is a two-way street. Listening is just as critical as asking for advice. Sometimes, we go into conversations with mentors already expecting a particular answer, which can close us off to new perspectives. Give your mentors the space to share their thoughts fully, even if their feedback challenges your assumptions. Pay attention not only to their words but also to what might not be said—nonverbal cues and subtle forms of communication can provide additional insight. Don't overthink it, but being attuned to these signals can be valuable.

Asking the right questions is equally important. Vague or overly broad questions can lead to unhelpful advice. Instead of asking, "What should I do?" try something more specific, like, "What would you recommend I consider when making this decision?" This approach invites your mentor to provide more focused and thoughtful guidance, giving you advice that's truly useful.

Practically speaking, you should always communicate professionally! By this, I mean you should write thank-you notes and follow up on conversations. Do so however you typically communicate with that mentor, whether by email, text, phone, or snail mail. Stay on top of the back-and-forth communications. If they reach out, get right back to them. You may have heard it said that the busiest people are the best at getting things done and returning your calls or texts. This is very true in my experience. It was impressive how one of my mentors (a billionaire and chairman of multiple companies) would always call me back the same day I called him. It was astonishing, really, and was a great example. There was one time he didn't get back to me for two weeks. I was worried I had offended him or something was wrong. Eventually, he called me apologetically and said he was fighting off a hostile takeover of one of his companies from a more prominent company (a $100 billion organization). I told him, "That was the best excuse I ever heard!" And that he didn't owe me an apology! So if he can be that good at getting back to a then twenty-something year old, you can be too!

A great book that can be helpful in this area is *How to Talk to Anyone: 92 Little Tricks for Big Success in Relationships* by Leil Lowndes.

INITIATIVE AND COMMITMENT

Both the mentor and mentee play active roles in fostering growth and collaboration. As a mentee, taking initiative and demonstrating commitment is key to building a strong, meaningful mentorship. Managing the relationship proactively is a big part of showing initiative. Scheduling meetings ahead of time and aligning with your mentor's availability shows that you respect their time and are serious about the process. Instead of waiting for your mentor to follow up, take responsibility for following up on action items from previous conversations. This keeps the momentum going and shows your dedication to applying their advice in meaningful ways. It also helps your mentor feel personally invested in your success, making them a stakeholder.

One helpful strategy is to calendar your interactions for the year. You don't have to stick to it rigidly, but it serves as a useful reminder to check in with your mentor at different points throughout the year. It's also a great place to note their birthdays, important milestones, or anything unique about them. Taking the time to do this will make you stand out, and mentors will appreciate your thoughtfulness and effort. They're more likely to stay engaged and supportive when they see your genuine commitment.

Preparation is another essential part of showing initiative. Before each meeting, take time to prepare a clear agenda, thoughtful questions, or updates on your progress. Whether you're tackling a specific challenge, sharing feedback, or seeking advice on a new opportunity, having focused topics ensures that your time together is productive. Doing research on your mentor or their organization can also help you frame your discussions better.

Mentors often have demanding schedules, so demonstrating that you're proactive and organized makes their role more fulfilling. It also builds trust and credibility in your relationship, as they see that their time and advice are truly valued. When mentors feel valued, they're more likely to go above and beyond in supporting your efforts.

Ultimately, showing initiative and commitment creates a dynamic and goal-oriented mentorship. It transforms the relationship from a passive exchange of advice into a collaborative journey where both mentor and mentee feel engaged, motivated, and invested in each other's success.

FEEDBACK AND CRITICISM

One of the most valuable aspects of having a mentor is receiving feedback that helps you grow. But let's face it—hearing criticism, even when it's constructive, isn't always easy. The key is to approach feedback with an open mind and a willingness to learn. When your mentor offers advice or highlights areas for improvement, listen carefully, reflect on it, and apply what you can. Being open to criticism is essential for growth; the more you embrace it, the easier it becomes over time.

For instance, if your mentor suggests improving your presentation skills, try responding with something like, "That's a great point—I hadn't thought about it that way. I'll work on refining my messaging and would appreciate your feedback on my next presentation." This kind of openness shows that you value their input and are committed to getting better.

I've experienced this firsthand. One of my professors was often very blunt with her critiques of me and my work. While it wasn't always easy to hear, her honesty became incredibly valuable to me. You can't improve if you're unable to see and address your areas of weakness. I've come to value people like her—those who are willing to be direct with me. Eventually, I've built deep trust with mentors and friends who feel free to hold me accountable and share honest, unfiltered perspectives.

That said, I have personal boundaries for this level of feedback (as you should too). It's something I reserve for people who've earned my trust and a place in my life. Only my closest friends can approach me with unvarnished critiques. Maintaining these boundaries ensures that the feedback I receive is constructive and comes from a place of genuine care.

RESPECT AND RECIPROCITY

A strong mentor-mentee relationship is built on mutual respect and a sense of balance. Respect lays the foundation for trust, while reciprocity helps maintain the connection. Even though mentors are often more experienced or knowledgeable, there are still plenty of ways you can give back—sometimes through small, thoughtful gestures.

Supporting your mentors doesn't have to involve grand acts. Small efforts can mean a lot. For example, one of my mentors had a deep passion for history, especially the Civil War era. When I came across a book on Abraham Lincoln, I sent him a copy. It wasn't just about the book—it was the thought behind it. It showed that I valued his interests and our relationship.

These relationships naturally grow stronger when you take the time to consider your mentor's needs and interests. Paying attention to what's important to them and finding ways to reciprocate, even in small ways, helps ensure that the relationship remains meaningful and mutually beneficial. Another instance, if I noticed something that aligned with a mentor's interests—a place they'd mentioned traveling to or a subject they were passionate about—I'd send them a postcard or a thoughtful note. Simple gestures, like sending a birthday or holiday card, can go a long way in keeping the relationship alive and showing you care.

It's important to remember, though, that *authenticity is key*. People at this level are often very skilled at reading others. If your motivation for building these relationships is purely self-serving, mentors will sense it. Approaching the connection as a stepping stone to something else won't help you in the long run. My goal has always been to encourage others to connect with more experienced, knowledgeable, and successful individuals—not as a way to climb the social ladder, but as a way to learn, grow, and become better themselves.

When your intentions are genuine and you're committed to both your and your mentor's growth, professional advancement tends to follow naturally as a by-product. However, if your sole focus is on advancing your career without genuinely valuing the relationships you're building, this approach isn't for you.

Building authentic relationships with mentors means being honest, transparent, and genuinely invested in the connection. It's about creating a bond rooted in mutual respect, trust, and a shared commitment to growth. When you approach mentorship with this mindset, you create something far more meaningful than just a professional network—you create relationships that can enrich your life in unexpected ways.

TRUST THROUGH AUTHENTICITY

Building a meaningful mentor-mentee relationship starts with authenticity. By being honest about your goals, showing genuine interest, and respecting boundaries, you create a foundation of trust and mutual growth. Authenticity strengthens the connection, allowing for deeper guidance, more valuable feedback, and a more impactful mentorship experience.

Be Honest About Your Goals and Challenges

- Clearly communicate what you hope to achieve and where you need guidance.
- Don't exaggerate your strengths or hide your weaknesses. Mentors can only help if they have an accurate picture of your situation.

Show Genuine Interest in Their Experiences

- Take the time to learn about your mentor's journey, values, and perspectives.
- Demonstrate authentic curiosity and gratitude for the time and wisdom they share.

Bring Your True Self

- Share your authentic personality, including your ambitions, fears, and unique qualities.
- Avoid pretending to be someone you're not to impress them. Mentors value honesty over perfection.

Build Trust Through Consistency

- Follow through on commitments, whether it's completing tasks they've suggested or showing up prepared for meetings.
- Trust is built over time by being reliable and consistent in your actions.

Respect Boundaries and Time

- Be mindful of their limits and respect their personal and professional boundaries.
- Authenticity doesn't mean overstepping or being overly familiar—it means valuing the relationship enough to maintain professionalism.

Be Open to Feedback

- Accept constructive criticism with an open mind and a willingness to improve.
- Authenticity involves humility and the ability to grow from their insights.

Practice Gratitude

- Express genuine appreciation for their guidance and support.
- Acknowledge the impact they have on your journey, both in words and actions.

Give Back When You Can

- Authentic relationships are two-way streets. While you may not be able to offer the same level of expertise, find ways to add value, whether it's sharing your progress, supporting their initiatives, or paying it forward to others.

In essence, being authentic with your mentors means prioritizing sincerity and mutual growth over transactional interactions. It fosters a deeper, more meaningful relationship that benefits both you and your mentor.

RETHINKING THE JOURNEY

As you read this book, I'd like to suggest considering an alternative perspective: replacing the word "journey" with the word "dance" in certain contexts. While "journey" is a fitting metaphor in many cases and remains a key part of this book, there are moments where thinking of life as a "dance" can offer a fresh and inspiring perspective.

Life is often described as a journey—a path with a starting point, milestones to achieve, and a final destination. Along the way, we tend to focus on climbing ladders, reaching goals, and chasing success, often believing that fulfillment lies somewhere in the future. However, **Alan Watts,** a British philosopher and writer, invites us to see life not as a journey but as a dance. In this view, life isn't about arriving at a specific destination; it's about fully immersing ourselves in the present, savoring each moment, and finding joy in the rhythm of living.

Alan Watts explores this concept of life as a dance in his lectures and writings, especially in his book *The Taboo Against*

Knowing Who You Are (often referred to simply as *The Book*). In it, he emphasizes experiencing life as a dynamic process, much like a piece of music or a dance, where the value lies in the experience itself—not in reaching an endpoint.

When it comes to mentorship and building a Board of Directors for Life, this metaphor takes on new meaning. A journey can sometimes feel rigid, with fixed plans and outcomes, where mentors are seen as guides to help us reach specific goals. But if life is a dance, mentors become more than guides—they are partners, teachers, and even co-creators who help us move with greater grace, confidence, and spontaneity.

Dancing with Your Mentors

In a dance, every step is intentional, yet there's space for improvisation, collaboration, and flow. Similarly, mentorship isn't just about achieving specific goals; it's about engaging in a dynamic exchange of ideas, values, and wisdom that shapes who you are in the moment. Here's how the metaphor connects to mentorship:

- **Fluidity Over Rigidity:** Mentors help you adapt to the unexpected rhythms of life. They teach you to approach challenges with resilience and curiosity, seeing change not as a threat but as part of the dance.
- **Being Present:** Great mentors remind you of the importance of being present—not just planning but also appreciating the steps you're taking right now. They show you that growth isn't just about reaching outcomes; it's about the discoveries you make along the way.
- **Joy in the Process:** Just like a dance is meant to be enjoyed, mentorship is about finding meaning

and joy in the learning process. Mentors celebrate your small wins and guide you to see the value in the experience itself, even when the ultimate goal isn't yet clear.

Mentorship as a Collaborative Dance

In the dance of life, mentors don't dictate your steps; they guide, encourage, and refine them. They share stories of their own time on the dance floor—the missteps, the lessons, and the rhythms they've learned to master. Their role isn't to steer you toward a specific end but to help you move through life with purpose and grace.

Thinking of life as a dance also shifts the focus of mentorship away from being solely about achieving results. Instead, it becomes about enrichment, growth, and finding joy in the moment. Your Board of Directors for Life is there to enhance your rhythm, broaden your perspective, and help you create a dance that's uniquely yours. Together, you and your mentors can choreograph a dynamic, fulfilling experience—one that's not about racing to the finish line but about enjoying the beauty of the performance as it unfolds.

Questions to journal on...

How can you show genuine appreciation for a mentor's time and guidance, and what specific steps can you take to maintain regular communication with them?

When did you receive criticism from a mentor that ended up benefiting you?

Chapter Challenge: Take a moment to reflect on who in your life has shaped your values and guided your decisions.

Instagram, Substack and X @yourboard4life
#chapter5challenge #yourboard4life

CHAPTER 6

LEVERAGING YOUR BOARD FOR SUCCESS

- **Maximizing influence:** Leveraging your board's collective wisdom to navigate challenges and seize opportunities. Mentors can help with critical decision-making, career transitions, and personal growth.
- **Your sphere of influence:** Leveraging mentorship and influence isn't about rank but about using relationships, credibility, and leadership to create meaningful impact and opportunities.

BUILDING A BOARD OF STAKEHOLDERS TO AMPLIFY YOUR IMPACT

I've learned to leverage my board of advisors to support projects and causes that matter to me. One of my mentors once said, "After your run for office, you have all this community support—maximize it." That advice sparked a shift in how I thought about my growing network that shaped my thinking from then on. It encouraged me to explore ways to use my influence to serve my community and expand my impact for the greater good.

As I reflect throughout this book, most of the stories I share focus on my early years because that's when I began building the foundations for what came later with regard to building my board of directors. I started small. For instance, I heard about a Model UN trip to Boston for the Harvard UN Simulation and immediately thought it would be an amazing educational opportunity. Seven other students were interested in going, but the university didn't have the budget to fund it. Determined to make it happen, I decided to raise the $10,000-plus that we needed. With guidance and support from my mentors, we raised more than enough in a short time.

I asked the university to make a nominal contribution to the trip. During a finance meeting, the board asked the dean of students if they thought the university would ultimately need to provide the funds. In other words, they wanted to know the likelihood of the students (primarily me) raising most of the necessary money, given that we only had about two weeks to do so. The dean replied that it was unlikely the university would need to match our raise. At the time, the university's dean didn't believe we could raise the required amount. However, I did—raising not only what was needed, but even more. The dean took notice of me, and he and I forged a great mentor-mentee relationship. Later the dean asked me to help raise an endowment, and I ended up doing so with the help of one donor I knew who no one had ever asked for a donation. The dean later awarded me a scholarship for my contribution to the university.

Those successes were eye-opening and got me thinking about how to make an even bigger impact. Around the same time, I learned about a low-income housing program the city was working on. They were applying for a federal grant to pilot the project. Seeing an opportunity to help, I got involved by organizing service providers and contractors willing to donate their time and skills. I also recruited a group of volunteers. The collaboration saved so much money that the city was able to renovate twice as many homes as originally planned. In turn, I made sure the service providers received well-deserved publicity for their contributions. The program ended up winning several awards, which was incredibly gratifying.

A couple of years later, after returning from London where I worked with the British Parliament, I found another way to bring people together by creating educational speaking tours in the U.S. for members of Parliament. With the backing of my advisors, corporate sponsors, and foundations, I was able to organize these events in a way that was meaningful for everyone involved. The tours provided an opportunity for my mentors and network to engage in something educational and personally interesting while also benefiting the community, the university, and international trade groups. It felt great to see these efforts contribute to strengthening Anglo-American relations while leveraging my network to make it all happen. All this while I was still in my early twenties.

Each of these experiences taught me valuable lessons and allowed me to expand my reach and sphere of influence a little more each time. With the help of my mentors, I was able to take on increasingly meaningful projects and make a real difference. I was thanking a mentor/funder of one of my projects, and he said to me that he didn't view what he was doing as all that much—he was "just writing a check." He said, "You were doing all this work and creating all these projects. That's the hard part." That is when I realized that I don't need to be wealthy to create change and make a difference—I can utilize other people's resources to make a difference. Very empowering...learning to leverage my mentors to increase my sphere of influence.

GIVING FIRST, ASKING LAST

I can't help but think about the famous marketing and business guru Gary Vaynerchuk, who talks about his principle of "Jab, Jab, Jab, Right Hook."

Gary's phrase "Jab, Jab, Jab, Right Hook" is a boxing metaphor that describes a strategic approach to social media marketing and building relationships with an audience. Here's what he means by it:

Jab, Jab, Jab

The "jabs" represent giving value to your audience without asking for anything in return. This could include:

- sharing useful information;
- providing entertaining or engaging content;
- offering tips, tutorials, or advice; and
- responding to comments and fostering genuine interactions.

The goal of the "jabs" is to build trust, goodwill, and a strong connection with your audience. By consistently delivering value, you demonstrate that you're invested in their interests and needs.

Right Hook

The "right hook" symbolizes the "ask" or the sale. It's the moment when you ask your audience to take a specific action, such as:

- buying a product or service;
- signing up for a newsletter;
- attending an event or webinar; or
- supporting a cause or campaign.

The "right hook" needs to be strategic, well-timed, and clear. It works best when it follows a series of value-packed "jabs" because the audience is more likely to respond positively when they've already received value from you.

Although it pertains to sales more than mentorship, it is an interesting concept to consider. I tend to be one who Jab, Jab, Jabs but is slower to Right Hook. In other words, I tend to focus on the serving part and not the "ask"—at least, not for personal gain. For the gain of others, I will make the ask and am unashamed to do so.

The Balance

Vaynerchuk emphasizes the importance of balancing jabs and hooks. Too many right hooks without enough jabs can alienate your audience, making them feel like they're only being sold something. On the other hand, endless jabs without ever delivering a right hook can leave opportunities on the table. The key is to give generously before making an ask, ensuring the relationship is reciprocal and mutually beneficial.

Real-Life Example

> **Jabs:** A fitness brand posts free workout tips, motivational content, and quick exercise videos.
>
> **Right Hook:** The brand launches a paid fitness app and asks followers to subscribe.

In essence, "Jab, Jab, Jab, Right Hook" is about understanding your audience's needs, building a relationship through value, and then strategically asking for their support when the time is right. For much more on this concept, check out Gary's book *Jab, Jab, Jab, Right Hook: How to Tell Your Story in a Noisy Social World.*

LEVERAGING YOUR SPHERE

During my journey, especially while I was still in college, I learned how to leverage the relationships I had with my mentors to create positive changes in my community. My goal wasn't intentionally about personal gain but about expanding my sphere of influence—something that, in turn, naturally supported my professional growth as well. This process deepened my connections with my advisors, giving them a chance to know me better while also offering me insights into how they operated. Essentially, I made them stakeholders in my life.

These relationships were mutually beneficial. They allowed me to grow as an individual while also making a meaningful impact on the world around me. Over the years, I've continued to use the knowledge, experience, and network I built with my

Small Sphere, Big Impact: Influence Is What You Make of It

Everyone has a sphere of influence—some large, some small. I'm particularly impressed by those who use their personal sphere to make a meaningful difference.

Take the service manager at my local BMW dealership, Jerod, for example, a man I truly admire who has maximized and leveraged his influence and authority for the benefit of others.

Although Jerod is a mid-level manager, he became the unofficial leader of the dealership due to his genuine concern for others. He intuitively understood his influence over those in his office and used it to uplift people. He was clever in managing his team, knew how to pick individuals with potential, and helped them move up or move on. He served as a buffer between employees and upper management, providing invaluable counsel up and down the chain of command.

Jerod was universally liked at the dealership because everyone knew how much he cared, and his advice was always solid. He was the glue that held the business together. After he left, there was a noticeable decline in morale, and the service center went from being one of the most profitable in the country to something far short of that. The atmosphere became so negative that I even began taking my car elsewhere because the level of service had declined so sharply.

To me, Jerod is a prime example of how someone, despite having a seemingly small sphere of influence, can leverage it to make a significant impact. He mentored his fellow employees and even his bosses, proving that influence is not about rank but how you use the authority and relationships you build. I had the privilege of mentoring Jerod during his time at BMW and watching him grow was an inspiration.

mentors to develop larger and more significant causes and projects. From setting up book and movie deals to building start-ups, raising millions for hundreds of nonprofits, and facilitating the release of prominent refugees, my sphere of influence has grown considerably.

That said, not everyone needs to have the same kind of sphere of influence. What matters is how you use the connections and resources available to you, no matter where you are in life. You can create a meaningful impact right where you are, starting small and building from there.

LEVERAGING YOUR CREDIBILITY AND PROBLEM-SOLVING

My mentors played a significant role in my life for over two decades. During that time, I accumulated countless stories of how they supported and guided me. Having this group of trusted advisors behind me as I advanced in life and my career gave me a confidence I might not have had otherwise. It empowered me to feel comfortable at any table, no matter the audience. Their networks were also extraordinary and opened doors I couldn't have accessed alone.

One key lesson I learned was how to ethically borrow my mentors' credibility in various situations. Knowing when and how to do this can be nuanced, and while I can't cover every scenario here, I'll share some guiding principles. Whenever I introduced a new idea or project, I'd often secure buy-in from one of my advisors first, gaining their support based on clear expectations and benchmarks.

For instance, when I began fundraising for the British tours to promote Anglo-American relations, which featured members of Parliament as speakers, I asked one of my mentors—a bank CEO—if he would sponsor the initiative. He agreed, on the condition that I raise the remaining funds from other organizations. With his commitment in hand, I approached other potential sponsors, saying, "I have a commitment from my bank CEO mentor for this amount, and I need your pledge to cover a portion." By leveraging his credibility, I demonstrated that he was already a stakeholder in the project, which gave both me and the initiative additional legitimacy. It also taught me how to be collaborative, which continues to serve me well.

This is an example of borrowing someone's credibility ethically. A good rule of thumb is to always ask for permission before using someone's name or commitment to support a project.

FROM CHALLENGES TO SOLUTIONS: THE MENTORSHIP ADVANTAGE

Many of my mentors' contributions involved sensitive professional situations that required confidentiality, so some stories will have to wait until later in life to be shared. However, I can say with confidence that having their support at such a young age gave me the courage to navigate challenges I never thought possible. This has been incredibly empowering.

One memorable instance I can share that's a bit more recent was when I was representing Mariam Ibraheem, a renowned refugee who was sentenced to execution by the Sudanese government for apostasy but rescued with the help of an organization where I served as chair of the board, and with additional help from Pope Francis and a few NGO's. When Mariam arrived in the United States, I coordinated an interview for her on Fox's *The Kelly File* with Megyn Kelly, at the time the highest-rated news show in America. We were set to travel to New York City for the interview on the same day—Mariam from Boston, and I from California.

Just before my flight, I learned that Mariam wouldn't be allowed to board hers because she didn't have any form of identification. Homeland Security had allowed her into the U.S. due to her unique refugee status, but she hadn't been issued an ID. Acting quickly, I reached out to various advisors. Through their connections with public interest groups, we got the Speaker of the House involved, who contacted the head of Homeland Security to request an exception to TSA regulations to let Mariam travel. By that evening, Mariam was able to fly to New York, and she completed her prime-time interview as planned—all coordinated via email from the plane. No small feat!

Later that week, Mariam and I were scheduled to attend Larry Page's Google Zeitgeist in Scottsdale, Arizona, where she would share a stage with former president Jimmy Carter and meet with former president Bill Clinton. The ID issue arose again, but this time, the favor from the Speaker couldn't be repeated. I had to find another solution—quickly. Despite reaching out to numerous government agencies, including the State Department and Homeland Security, and even consulting with immigration lawyers, I was told it would be impossible to resolve the issue in time. But one thing my mentors—and especially my mom—had taught me was to be a relentless problem solver. I refused to take no for an answer.

After much thought, I realized that undocumented individuals could obtain state IDs in some places. Why couldn't Mariam? I researched and connected with the office of a U.S. senator from New Hampshire, where Mariam lived. They coordinated with the DMV in Manchester to issue her a state ID. By Friday at 5:00 p.m.—just as the DMV was closing—everything was finalized, and just as my flight was landing back in Santa Barbara, California, from New York City. Mariam, her family, and I were able to fly to Arizona early the next morning, arriving in time for Larry Page's Google Zeitgeist weekend.

This experience reinforced the value of perseverance, creativity, and the network I had built with the help of my mentors. They not only taught me how to solve problems but also gave me the tools to leverage relationships to help others in meaningful ways.

STAKEHOLDERS BECOME STAY-HOLDERS

Another example of leveraging my mentors came when I supported a youth-focused nonprofit. A couple of friends had started a nonprofit youth center in Wisconsin in the early 2000s, and although it was only about a year old, they had big ambitions. They wanted to raise funds to provide computers and create an event space for teenagers in the community. I saw an opportunity to help and introduced one of my mentors to their project. This mentor was on the board of several foundations, and I hoped to gain his buy-in.

We toured the site together, and my friends shared their vision for what they wanted to create. While their enthusiasm was inspiring, they had made some early missteps in the community—unintentionally stepping on toes of other similar organizations. Their eagerness had left them a bit blind to the political landscape, which is why I wanted to step in—not just because I cared about their mission, but because I wanted to help them navigate past these challenges.

When my mentor visited, he offered thoughtful and reasonable suggestions for improvements, though they would take some time to implement—potentially months. The team worked diligently on those changes, and once everything was in place, we approached him again to share the progress we had made. Seeing their commitment to following through on his recommendations encouraged him and made a strong impression. Afterward, I officially applied for a grant from one of his foundations, highlighting the improvements and reminding him of his earlier involvement.

The nonprofit was awarded the grant, and it was clear that we had achieved more than just securing funding—we had created a sense of investment for my mentor in the nonprofit's governance and future success. In fact, he asked a lawyer from his law firm to serve on their board so he could provide ongoing advice and oversight. By leveraging this relationship thoughtfully, the organization gained a long-term supporter. My mentor didn't just become a stakeholder—he became a stay-holder.

These are just a few examples, but they underscore an important lesson I've learned: Leveraging knowledge and skill sets is key. While I may not be an expert in every area I operate in, I've surrounded myself with people whose expertise complements my own. Through my mentors, I've gained insights into corporate law, banking, insurance, technology, public policy, entrepreneurship, negotiation, perseverance, and more. These tools have been critical to my success—not just in business, but in life. Additionally, I have made my mentors stakeholders in a variety of my decisions as well. This creates a powerful connection that keeps them engaged and demonstrates appreciation and value for their efforts.

Navigating Disagreements with Mentors

Sometimes, following your mentor's guidance just isn't possible. Maybe their advice doesn't align with your vision, or maybe external constraints—like funding priorities, organizational structure, or long-term strategy—make it unworkable. In the nonprofit world, this kind of misalignment is often referred to as "mission creep"—when an organization starts drifting away from its core purpose in pursuit of funding, partnerships, or external expectations. While it might seem like a smart short-term move, it can dilute the mission, confuse stakeholders, and ultimately weaken the organization's impact. It's like trying to make everyone at a dinner party happy by serving sushi, barbecue, and spaghetti all at once. Instead of satisfying anyone, you just end up with a confusing mess.

So, what do you do when you can't follow the direction your mentor—or, in this case, a donor—wants?

The key is to negotiate whenever possible. Instead of approaching the situation as an all-or-nothing decision, look for areas of alignment. Can you find a compromise that respects their input while keeping your vision intact? Can you adapt their advice in a way that still serves your goals? Many times, a small shift in perspective can turn what feels like a conflict into an opportunity for collaboration.

But sometimes, a true compromise isn't possible. In those cases, you have to be willing to walk away from the opportunity—but not from the mentor. The relationship is bigger than this one decision. Let them know that while you can't act on their advice in this

FROM MANY COUNSELORS, WISDOM FLOWS

Once you've assembled your personal board of advisors, the next step is learning how to effectively use their guidance when making decisions. This process varies depending on the situation, the mentor, and the mentee, but there are foundational principles that can help. I developed my own decision-making process in my early teens, inspired by the idea of seeking wisdom from many counselors. As someone who values objectivity and rationality, this concept resonated deeply with me.

A guiding principle I've always lived by is *veritas*—the Latin word for truth. To me, everything flows from this foundation. To uncover truth, I make it a point to thoroughly research topics, often starting with books, reliable online resources, and other materials. However, I've learned that the most impactful approach goes beyond gathering information—it's about seeking out experts and learning from their personal experiences. Hearing how they've applied their knowledge, navigated decisions, and dealt with both successes and failures offers perspectives that you can't always find in a book.

Ultimately, experience is key. Early on, I recognized the value of surrounding myself with a diverse group of experts and counselors who filled in the "gaps" or areas where I needed expertise. (More on decision-making in the next chapter.)

instance, you deeply value their insight, guidance, and support. A great mentor—or a thoughtful donor, as in this example—will respect your commitment to your vision, even if they don't agree with every choice you make.

At the end of the day, this isn't just about protecting an organization's mission—it's about developing your own leadership and decision-making skills. A mentor's role is to provide wisdom and perspective, but your role is to filter that advice through your own vision, values, and goals. Learning to navigate these moments with confidence and integrity isn't just about keeping a relationship intact—it's about becoming the kind of leader who can make tough calls while staying true to themselves.

FROM THE ICE TO LIFE: APOLO OHNO'S BLUEPRINT FOR MENTORSHIP

Apolo Ohno is truly an inspirational figure. As the most decorated American in Winter Olympics history, with an impressive total of eight medals, he embodies extraordinary achievement. Beyond his athletic success, Apolo profoundly understands the importance of building a Board of Directors for Life.

In his recently published book *Hard Pivot,* Apolo discusses this very concept. He introduces his personal "Starting Five"—a trusted inner circle of mentors, coaches, and accountability partners who have played pivotal roles in his journey. These individuals are not just advisors; they are people Apolo has carefully chosen to guide, challenge, and support him through life's transitions and decisions.

The story of Apolo Ohno's father, Yuki, offers an inspiring example of how the people closest to us can profoundly shape our lives. For Apolo, his father wasn't just a parent—he was a cornerstone of his personal board. Yuki ran a hair salon in Seattle, Washington, and was a single parent to Apolo after divorcing his mother when Apolo was an infant. Yuki was dedicated to his son and would drive hundreds of miles to take Apolo to rollerblading competitions early on, and later ice-skating ones. He devoted his entire life to raising his son. Yuki's life story is one of resilience, self-sacrifice, and wisdom, and it reminds us how essential it is to have people in our corner who guide us with strength and integrity.

Yuki's example resonates deeply because it illustrates the type of person we should strive to have on our board. These people are selfless; they give without expecting anything in return, and challenge us to grow professionally, emotionally, and spiritually.

Expanding the Circle

Apolo didn't stop at his father—his board included people who brought completely different skills to the table. For instance, he credits **John Schaeffer,** a powerlifting coach, with revolutionizing his training regimen in the lead-up to the 2010 Olympics. John had no skating experience but helped Apolo reshape his body and mind for optimal performance.

This is an important reminder for all of us: Your board should include people with perspectives and expertise different from your own. Whether it's a mentor who's mastered a skill you want to develop, a friend who holds you accountable, or someone who challenges you to see the world in a new way, their influence can stretch you in ways you might not have thought possible.

In my life, I've found that the most impactful people are those who bring a mix of practical advice and emotional support. Some will guide you with structured frameworks, like Apolo's friend **Doug Jowdy's** focus on sports psychology and visualization, while others will introduce useful tools, as when Apolo's psychologist, **David Creswell,** taught him the value of journaling and mindfulness. The common thread among these people? They expand your capabilities while helping you stay grounded in who you are.

The Risk of Poor Choices

Not all people who enter your life will have your best interests at heart. Apolo shared his experience of investing in a flashy real estate group that ultimately over-leveraged themselves and went bankrupt, costing him millions of dollars and crushing him emotionally. It's a sobering reminder that diligence matters.

The people you choose for your board of directors should be vetted with care, whether in business, personal life, or even friendships. Ask yourself: Do these individuals truly support my growth? Will they challenge me constructively when I need it most? We can all learn from Apolo's misstep in trusting the wrong people. Success isn't just about talent or hard work—it's also about surrounding yourself with the right people.

When I think of a professional athlete like Apolo Ohno, I'm reminded of the tremendous discipline it takes to achieve the goal of becoming an Olympian, let alone an eight-time medalist. This serves as a powerful reminder of the importance of creating transformative habits.

Apolo asked me to emphasize the importance of "Building a support system that is both beneficial to your professional growth and personal life, as well as a critical piece to increasing your outcomes and success rate...build it [your support system] wisely". Whether it's going to the gym regularly, reading daily, eating healthy, meditating, or even something as simple as making your bed, these actions build habits that contribute to your overall success. Long-term, these habits can not only improve your life but also foster the relationships that help you grow and advance you personally and professionally.

Questions to journal on...

How can you better leverage the relationships and networks you already have to create a greater impact in your personal or professional life?

Are you effectively making your mentors and advisors stakeholders in your journey, or are you simply seeking advice without fostering long-term engagement? What steps can you take to build credibility and trust with your mentors, so they become invested in your success for the long-term?

Chapter Challenge: Have you ever faced a challenge where mentorship or guidance from your board of directors helped you succeed? If so, what lessons did you learn from the experience?

Instagram, Substack and X @yourboard4life
#chapter6challenge #yourboard4life

CHAPTER 7

DECISION-MAKING WITH MENTORS

- **Harnessing the power of intuition:** Understanding how intuition works and why it is a valuable decision-making tool.
- **Journaling—creating a feedback loop for intuition:** Using journaling to track and refine your instincts for better judgment in the long run.
- **The role of emotional intelligence in decision-making:** Strengthening intuition through self-awareness, empathy, and emotional regulation.
- **Balancing mentor advice with personal instincts:** Integrating external guidance with your own intuition to make well-informed and confident decisions.

SHARPENING YOUR INNER COMPASS

One of the challenges people often face is finding the right balance between critical analysis, deferring to authority, and trusting their intuition. Among these, intuition tends to be the most underdeveloped skill for many.

Intuition, often referred to as a "gut feeling," is a powerful yet sometimes overlooked tool in decision-making. It's not just a mystical sense—it's your brain's ability to process and synthesize thousands of subtle data points all at once, even if your conscious mind hasn't yet categorized or articulated them. This is especially important when you're still building experience or exposure to specific patterns. Sometimes, your instincts are spot on; other times, they might miss the mark. Either way, these outcomes are opportunities to learn how to develop and refine your intuition.

One practice I encourage for mentees is to journal their major decisions. This helps cultivate trust in their intuition. As you journal, take note of the feelings or instincts you had at the time of the decision—particularly your initial perceptions of people and situations. In due course, as you review your notes, patterns will begin to emerge. You'll start to see where your instincts aligned with reality and where they didn't. This reflection process not only builds confidence in your intuition but also provides a concrete way to validate and sharpen it.

WHY PEOPLE IGNORE INTUITION

Many people dismiss their intuition for three main reasons:

1. **Lack of Categorization:** When you can't clearly articulate or explain the basis for your feelings, it's tempting to disregard them.
2. **Groupthink and Peer Pressure:** External influences, such as a desire to conform or defer to authority, can overshadow your internal cues.
3. **Lack of Confidence:** People don't have the tools or experience in utilizing their intuition to feel confident in depending on it more.

However, ignoring intuition can lead to missed opportunities or mistakes. Instead, I suggest embracing these feelings, even when they aren't immediately explainable, and treating them as a piece of the decision-making puzzle.

Two great books to help jump-start your intuitive process are *Read People Like a Book: How to Analyze, Understand, and Predict People's Emotions, Thoughts, Intentions, and Behaviors* by Patrick King and *The Secrets of Body Language: An Illustrated Guide to Knowing What People Are Really Thinking and Feeling* by Philippe Turchet.

JOURNALING: BUILDING A FEEDBACK LOOP

Journaling is essential for honing your intuitive skills. Over time, you'll notice that the "unexplainable" becomes explainable as you recognize recurring patterns and learn to categorize experiences. This process allows you to develop a sharper sense of perception and ultimately make better, faster decisions.

When journaling:

- Note your initial gut reactions and how you felt during the decision-making process.
- Reflect on the outcome of your decisions and how closely they matched your initial instincts.
- Analyze any missteps to understand where your intuition may have led you astray and consider what factors might have influenced your perception.

This practice creates a feedback loop, helping you fine-tune your intuition and improving your confidence in your own judgment.

INTUITION AS A SKILL AND A SUPERPOWER

Intuition is a skill that everyone possesses to varying degrees, and like any skill, it can be developed with practice and discipline. For some, it can even become a superpower—a finely tuned ability to read situations, assess people, and make sound decisions in real time.

Fine-Tuning Intuition to Strengthen Emotional Intelligence

Developing your intuition to enhance emotional intelligence is a process of self-discovery and meaningful connection. It starts with *self-awareness*. Picture yourself taking a quiet moment to reflect, maybe journaling about a time when you reacted strongly to something. As you explore the situation, patterns start to emerge—triggers, recurring emotions, and how they shaped your choices. Eventually, this practice helps you better understand your inner world, sharpening your ability to sense what feels right or wrong in various situations.

Next comes *empathy*. Imagine being fully present in a conversation, not just listening to respond but truly tuning in to the other person. You notice subtle shifts in their tone, their gestures, or even the way they pause between words. These nonverbal cues can reveal emotions that words might not express. As you practice this level of attention, your intuition about what others are feeling becomes clearer, deepening your connections and building stronger relationships.

Emotional regulation is another essential skill. Think of those moments of conflict when you want to react instantly—but instead, you pause. Taking a deep breath before responding creates space for your intuition to guide you toward a thoughtful reply rather than a reflexive reaction. It's like learning to steer a boat steadily through choppy waters—emotions may surge, but they no longer control your course.

These practices—self-awareness, empathy, and emotional regulation—work together progressively, shaping a more intuitive and emotionally intelligent version of yourself. Your instincts grow sharper, your responses become more thoughtful, and your relationships benefit as a result.

Integrating Intuition with Mentorship and Critical Thinking

Blending intuition with advice from mentors as well as your own critical analysis allows you to process guidance more effectively and think independently. This balanced approach helps you make decisions that are not only well-informed but also deeply aligned with your personal values and perceptions. Gradually, this combination becomes an invaluable skill that enhances both your professional success and personal fulfillment.

THE ROLE OF EMOTIONAL QUOTIENT

Emotional Quotient (EQ) is often what separates those who are successful from those who are truly exceptional. Many Fortune 400 CEOs emphasize that their most important skill isn't technical knowledge or strategy—it's social perceptivity.

EQ is the ability to recognize, understand, manage, and influence emotions—both your own and those of others. By honing your EQ, you not only improve how you relate to others but also refine how you navigate challenges and opportunities in both life and work.

Key components of EQ include:

- **Self-Awareness:** Recognizing and understanding your emotions and their impact on your behavior and decisions.
- **Self-Regulation:** Managing emotions in healthy ways, staying in control, and adapting to changing circumstances.
- **Motivation:** Using emotions to drive positive outcomes, maintain focus, and persist in achieving goals.
- **Empathy:** Understanding and sharing the feelings of others, fostering stronger relationships and collaboration.
- **Social Skills:** Navigating social interactions effectively, resolving conflicts, and inspiring others.

EQ is important in several ways:

- **Personal Development:** Enhances self-awareness and helps in managing stress and challenges.
- **Professional Success:** Essential for leadership, teamwork, and communication in the workplace.
- **Relationship Building:** Strengthens personal and professional relationships through understanding and connection.
- **Decision-Making:** Supports better judgment by balancing logic and emotions.

EQ is often considered as important as, if not more important than, traditional measures of intelligence (IQ) in determining success and well-being. It can be developed and improved over time through practice and reflection.

Timing of Mentor Involvement

In a mentor-mentee relationship, it's essential to determine when to seek mentor input.

- **Transactional Advice:** Mentors provide immediate, practical guidance for time-sensitive or situational decisions, such as drafting a contract, resolving a dispute, or addressing a short-term challenge.
- **Strategic Advice:** Mentors guide mentees in long-term planning, focusing on broader goals like career development, organizational strategy, or leadership growth. Understanding the nature of the decision ensures the mentor's input is appropriately utilized.

MENTOR ADVICE WITH PERSONAL INTUITION

While mentors can offer valuable insights based on their experiences, you know your situation, strengths, and goals best. An approach to explore here is a "weighing matrix," where mentees list the advice provided by each mentor, along with personal instincts and other relevant factors, to assess how they align or conflict. Here is how to create your own weighing matrix:

Break Down Each Mentor's Advice by Categories

When receiving advice from mentors, categorize their suggestions to ensure clarity and relevance. Examples of categories might include:

- **Feasibility:** Is the advice realistic given your current resources, skills, or circumstances?

Example: A mentor might suggest launching a start-up, but you may lack the financial stability or market research to take such a leap immediately.

- **Alignment with Long-Term Goals:** Does the advice support your overarching objectives?

  Example: If your goal is to gain management experience, advice to take a highly specialized technical role might not align with your broader aspirations.

- **Potential Risks:** What are the downsides or uncertainties associated with the advice?

  Example: A mentor could encourage a high-risk investment opportunity that might jeopardize your financial security.

By breaking advice into these categories, you can evaluate it more systematically.

Assign a Weight to Each Mentor's Advice

Evaluate each piece of advice based on the mentor's expertise in the relevant area. Assign higher weights to advice that aligns with their strengths and track record.

Example:

- Mentor A, a successful entrepreneur, suggests strategies for scaling your business. Assign their advice a higher weight when considering entrepreneurial decisions.

- Mentor B, a finance expert, advises caution on budgeting. Their advice gets a higher weight for financial decisions.

By prioritizing advice based on expertise, you can ensure that your decisions are informed by the most credible sources.

Compare Mentor Advice Against Personal Instincts

After evaluating mentor input, reflect on your own instincts and experiences. Use the weighing matrix to identify areas of synergy or conflict:

- **Synergies:** Look for advice that reinforces your instincts.

  Example: If multiple mentors suggest pursuing further education, and you also feel the need for upskilling, this synergy indicates a strong path forward.

- **Disparities:** Examine advice that conflicts with your instincts to identify blind spots or areas requiring deeper consideration.

  Example: A mentor might suggest accepting a demanding role for career growth, but your instincts signal a need for work-life balance. Weigh these conflicting priorities to determine the best course of action.

Visualization: The Weighing Matrix

Here's how a simple matrix might look in practice:

Mentor	Advice	Feasibility (1-5)	Alignment (1-5)	Risk (1-5)	Weighted Score
A	Pursue a start-up idea	3	5	2	10
B	Take a corporate leadership role	4	4	3	11
C	Invest in professional courses	5	5	1	11

This matrix allows you to quantify advice and instincts, leading to more balanced, data-informed decision-making.

VALUES-BASED GUIDANCE

Mentor advice should align with the mentee's values and long-term vision. Tools like value alignment checklists help mentees assess whether the advice supports their personal principles and organizational mission. This ensures that decisions, while informed by the mentor, remain authentic and true to the mentee's goals.

Reflection is key to maximizing the value of a mentor relationship and making sure it aligns with your values and goals. Mentees should regularly revisit past advice and evaluate the outcomes of decisions made with their mentor's input. Discussing these reflections with the mentor fosters deeper self-awareness, strengthens the relationship, and refines the mentee's approach to future challenges. It also promotes the concept of creating stakeholders out of your mentors and not just distant advisors.

GROUP DECISION-MAKING DYNAMICS

Some decisions are better made through group deliberation, especially when your mentors bring diverse perspectives to the table. You could expand on group-facilitation techniques for how to lead discussions among your board members to foster collaborative decision-making. This includes:

- **Structured Brainstorming:** Set up formal meetings with multiple mentors at once, facilitating a structured conversation where all viewpoints are shared openly before coming to a collective decision. I only recommend this once you have established these relationships over a prolonged period and for issues that are very significant. Convening your mentors all at one meeting should be a rare event. (I may have done this once in twenty years.)
- **Delphi Method:** This technique involves gathering anonymous input from each mentor independently, synthesizing the feedback, and then sharing a summary with the group to build consensus without the pressure of groupthink.

FROM CONFORMITY TO DIVERSITY: JFK'S LEADERSHIP EVOLUTION

Here is an example from history that shows how even presidents of the United States can make bad decisions and learn from them and then resist groupthink and save the world!

In the early 1960s, President John F. Kennedy navigated two defining moments in U.S. history that underscored the risks of groupthink in decision-making. The first was the Bay of Pigs invasion in 1961, a covert operation aimed at toppling Cuban leader Fidel Castro. Unfortunately, this plan revealed how overconfidence and a lack of critical debate among Kennedy's advisors led to flawed assumptions. Key voices of caution were subdued, as some advisors hesitated to challenge the prevailing consensus, creating a blind spot in the decision-making process.

Kennedy, new to the presidency, later reflected on how this atmosphere of conformity contributed to the operation's failure. He acknowledged that fostering a more open environment for debate and encouraging alternative perspectives might have led to better outcomes. The lessons from this experience shaped how he approached challenges moving forward.

When the Cuban Missile Crisis emerged in 1962, Kennedy applied these hard-earned insights to avoid repeating past mistakes. Faced with the potential for nuclear confrontation, he prioritized creating a more inclusive and deliberative decision-making process. This time, he encouraged his advisors to present diverse opinions and welcomed dissent, recognizing that constructive disagreement could strengthen decisions.

To further counter groupthink, Kennedy implemented several thoughtful strategies. He divided his advisory team into smaller groups, tasking them with independently evaluating different options. This approach minimized the dominance of any single viewpoint and allowed for more rigorous consideration of various strategies. He also took care to invite outside experts into the discussions, ensuring that fresh perspectives could challenge any entrenched biases.

Kennedy also emphasized the importance of patience and deliberation. Rather than rushing to a conclusion, he kept discussions open until the team reached a carefully considered decision. This process led to the implementation of a naval "quarantine" of Cuba, a measured response that opened the door for diplomatic negotiations rather than immediate military action.

The resolution of the Cuban Missile Crisis, which saw the peaceful withdrawal of Soviet missiles in exchange for U.S. assurances, showcased the effectiveness of Kennedy's revised leadership approach. By fostering open dialogue, encouraging diverse viewpoints, and thoughtfully weighing options, Kennedy successfully navigated one of the most dangerous moments in modern history.

This historical example highlights the risks of groupthink and the value of critical thinking and inclusivity in leadership. Kennedy's ability to learn from past challenges and adapt his decision-making approach was a turning point in his presidency, underscoring the power of embracing diverse perspectives in high-stakes situations.

INCORPORATING EXTERNAL FACTORS

Mentor advice is most effective when combined with an understanding of external influences. This includes tools such as SWOT analysis and scenario planning. These tools enrich decision-making by balancing mentor insights with external realities.

A SWOT analysis is a strategic framework used to assess an organization's (or an individual's) position by identifying and analyzing its strengths, weaknesses, opportunities, and threats (SWOT). Strengths and weaknesses represent internal factors—resources, capabilities, or challenges within the organization. Opportunities and threats are external factors, such as market trends, competition, or regulatory changes. By systematically evaluating these elements, organizations can capitalize on their strengths, address weaknesses, seize opportunities, and mitigate threats. This analysis provides a clear, structured approach to decision-making, strategy development, and problem-solving, making it an essential tool in business planning and competitive positioning.

Scenario planning is a strategic planning method that helps organizations (or individuals) anticipate and prepare for potential future uncertainties by exploring and analyzing various plausible scenarios. Instead of predicting one definitive outcome, it involves identifying key driving forces, trends, and uncertainties that could shape the future and developing detailed narratives or models around different potential futures. This approach allows businesses to evaluate how various strategies might perform under changing conditions, identify risks and opportunities, and create flexible plans. By considering a range of possibilities, scenario planning enhances an organization's adaptability, decision-making, and resilience in the face of uncertainty.

GOING IT ALONE

There have been times in my life when I had to "go it alone" and make decisions that went against both the advice of my mentors and the prevailing data. I touched on this in the previous chapter but wanted to explore this a bit more. One such instance was during the creation of my tech company, Polis Assist (www.polis-assist.com). Several experienced tech executives (not my personal board) told me it would be nearly impossible to find the coders I needed. They argued that coders were in such high demand that no one would be willing to work solely for equity, which was a key requirement for most of my company's partners.

On top of that, I was warned that collecting all the street-parking data for Los Angeles—a city with five hundred thousand blocks of street data—would be unfeasible. This data wasn't available digitally from the city or any other source, and my allo-

Navigating Power Without Compromise

An excellent book on decision-making, and one that has gained significant popularity, is *The 48 Laws of Power* by Robert Greene. It offers a fascinating historical exploration of power dynamics and strategies. However, I believe it's essential to approach this book with a critical eye, particularly regarding the ethical and moral implications of applying its wisdom. While the book is informative, it leans heavily on situational ethics and focuses solely on the acquisition of power, often disregarding the moral considerations of how that power is obtained.

In contrast, I advocate for the ethical acquisition of power and influence—power that is used in the service of others, aligned with the principles of servant leadership (a concept we'll get into more later). Some might argue that actions taken to secure or preserve power for the sake

cated budget for the project was seen as insufficient to achieve this task.

Despite these doubts, I chose to trust my instincts and comprehensive research and take a chance with my proprietary plan. In both cases, I proved them wrong. I successfully found talented coders willing to work for equity alone, and I managed to gather the parking data for LA within my very limited budget and predicted timeline.

These accomplishments continued to reinforce my belief that, while it's wise to seek advice and consider expert opinions, there are moments when trusting your intuition and taking a calculated risk is essential. While going against conventional wisdom shouldn't become a habit, sometimes you have to step out on your own and believe in your ability to succeed.

This experience underscored an important lesson: Even the best advice needs to be considered in the context of your own circumstances. Ultimately, there are times when we have to go it alone.

So, how do you decide when to go it alone?

Here are some things to consider:

Key Takeaways for Success in Going It Alone

Many of the people we read about from history or admire in the current zeitgeist are people who had to take the road less traveled. They had to, at certain points, go it alone and forge a new path. These are some of the secrets to their success:

- **Clarity of Vision:** Successful leaders often have a clear understanding of their goals and the impact they want to achieve.

of achieving a positive outcome can justify ethical or moral compromises. In essence, this argument suggests that the end justifies the means. However, this is a concept I reject in almost all circumstances.

While I acknowledge that there may be gray areas in certain situations, I firmly believe that the small decisions we make along the way are just as important as the desired outcome. The process matters as much as the result, and only by prioritizing both can we navigate a moral and ethical path for decision-making.

That said, I do recommend reading *The 48 Laws of Power* to understand the tools and strategies that might be employed by others, particularly adversaries or competitors. Awareness of these dynamics can be invaluable, but it's equally important to hold firm to one's own ethical principles while engaging with such wisdom.

- **Resilience and Adaptability:** They remain steadfast in the face of challenges and adjust strategies when needed.
- **Calculated Risks:** They weigh the risks and rewards of their decisions carefully, often using their resources strategically to gain an advantage.
- **Self-Belief:** They have confidence in their ideas and the willingness to bet on themselves, both crucial drivers of their success.
- **Experience:** They have knowledge and experience in most of the areas they are looking to work in—perhaps not all areas, but most.

Some books that could help you develop relationships that advance you include *How to Win Friends and Influence People* by Dale Carnegie, *The 7 Habits of Highly Effective People* by Stephen R. Covey, and *Developing the Leaders Around You: How to Help Others Reach Their Full Potential* by John C. Maxwell.

Questions to journal on...

When faced with a tough decision, how would you utilize your mentors' advice to weigh your options and align with your goals?

How can you ensure that the feedback from your mentors is synthesized effectively to avoid bad decision-making and build consensus?

Chapter Challenge: What is an example of a time when you had to make a tough decision, and what did you use to guide that process?

Instagram, Substack and X @yourboard4life
#chapter7challenge #yourboard4life

CHAPTER 8

THE ROLE OF EMOTIONAL AND MENTAL WELL-BEING

- **Support beyond professionalism:** A board of mentors guiding career growth while supporting emotional well-being, work-life balance, and stress management.

SEEKING EMOTIONAL SUPPORT IN MENTORSHIP

Seeking emotional support from your mentors or advisors is an important step in personal and professional growth. Approaching this with openness, respect, and clear communication helps create a balanced and supportive relationship. While a mentor's role can include guidance in many areas, it's important to remember they are not a substitute for professional mental health support. By being honest and patient and expressing gratitude, you can build a connection that respects both your needs and their boundaries.

Not all mentors are equipped to address every aspect of your journey, and that's okay. Some may focus primarily on professional advice, others on spiritual or emotional guidance. Each relationship will have its strengths. Some mentors might support you through a specific period or challenge, while others may offer their wisdom over many years. Understanding the unique strengths of each mentor and not placing unrealistic expectations on them is key to fostering a healthy dynamic.

Here are vital things to keep in mind when reaching out for emotional support from your advisors or mentors:

Recognize the Boundaries of Your Relationship

- **Understand their role:** Advisors/mentors are there to guide you, offer advice, and help with career and personal development. While many are compassionate and willing to provide emotional support, it's essential to recognize that they may not be equipped to handle serious mental health issues, and their focus may primarily be on your professional growth.
- **Know when to seek professional help:** If your emotional needs go beyond what a mentor can provide, seeking professional support, such as therapy or counseling, is essential. Mentors can offer guidance, but mental health professionals have the expertise to address more profound emotional challenges.

Be Open About Your Needs

- **Clarify what you're looking for:** Be up front about why you're seeking support. Are you seeking guidance on managing stress, improving work-life balance, or just a safe space to vent? Communicating your emotional needs allows your mentor to understand how they can best support you.

- **Set expectations:** While your mentor may be willing to listen and provide feedback, they may not have all the answers. It's helpful to be realistic about the emotional support you can expect.

Be Respectful of Their Time and Energy

- **Consider their availability:** Mentors are often busy professionals with their own responsibilities. Be mindful of their time and don't overwhelm them with frequent or prolonged requests for emotional support. Instead, schedule check-ins or meetings that are respectful of their commitments.
- **Gauge their willingness:** Not every mentor will have the bandwidth or emotional capacity to provide the level of support you may need at a given time. Pay attention to cues indicating their level of willingness to engage in emotionally supportive conversations and respect those boundaries.

Maintain Honesty and Transparency

- **Be honest about your struggles:** For the emotional support to be effective, you need to be open about what you're going through. Avoid downplaying your emotions or pretending everything is okay when it's not. Vulnerability is essential in creating a meaningful and supportive relationship.
- **Communicate your feelings:** If you feel uncomfortable with the direction of the conversation at any point, it's okay to express that. Mentorship is a

two-way street, and healthy communication is key to maintaining trust and respect.

Seek Support Without Overburdening Them

- **Balance emotional sharing:** While sharing what you're going through is important, avoid turning your meetings with your mentor into one-sided emotional unloading sessions. Try to balance the conversation with your professional growth and any personal matters.
- **Focus on career-related advice you might need:** This will prevent the relationship from feeling imbalanced or solely focused on emotional support.
- **Be mindful of frequency:** Regular check-ins are important, but make sure you're not overburdening your mentor with constant emotional support needs. Reach out when necessary, but also respect the nature of the relationship by ensuring it doesn't become exclusively about emotional support.

Understand That Mentors Are Human Too

- **Acknowledge their own limits:** Mentors may have emotional challenges of their own. Be mindful of their capacity to provide support, and don't expect them to be a constant emotional anchor. They may also need space to handle their own emotions and commitments.
- **Respect their boundaries:** Just as you may have emotional limits, so too do your mentors. They

might not always have the time, energy, or tools to support you in the way you need, and that's okay. If that's the case, it's essential to respect their limits and look for other sources of support, if necessary.

Be Open to Their Perspective

- **Accept feedback with an open mind:** Your mentor may offer insights or suggestions you hadn't considered. While the emotional support you seek may be more about validation, be open to receiving advice that may help you better manage your emotional well-being.
- **Consider constructive criticism:** Sometimes, emotional struggles are tied to deeper patterns in behavior or mindset that a mentor might identify. While it can be challenging to hear, constructive feedback can help you grow personally and professionally.

Maintain Professionalism and Respect

- **Respect professional boundaries:** Remember that your mentor is still in a professional role, and the relationship should maintain a certain level of professionalism. While it's okay to discuss emotional matters, keep the tone respectful and professional.
- **Maintain boundaries for personal disclosure:** It's okay to share personal challenges, but be mindful of how much you disclose. There's a balance between vulnerability and oversharing, and it's

essential to keep the mentorship relationship productive and grounded in mutual respect.

Express Gratitude for Their Support

- Acknowledge their efforts: Mentors offer their time, energy, and insights to help you. Expressing gratitude for their emotional support can help maintain a positive, reciprocal relationship.
- **Show appreciation in tangible ways:** You can show appreciation by following up with them on how their advice or support has impacted you. Whether you've made progress or have new questions, letting them know you value their guidance helps strengthen the relationship.

Consider the Timing and Context

- **Be mindful of timing:** Sometimes, it's better to address emotional issues at a time when both you and your mentor can give it the proper attention rather than during busy or stressful periods.
- **Context matters:** If the emotional issue is something personal, like a family loss or mental health struggle, consider whether this is something you want to discuss in the context of a mentorship session or whether it might be more appropriate to seek support elsewhere.

MINDFULNESS IN MENTORSHIP RELATIONSHIPS

Healthy mentorship is built on mutual respect, trust, and integrity. Occasionally, though rarely, inappropriate dynamics can arise, highlighting the need for vigilance. Grooming, where trust is misused for exploitation, serves as a reminder to always trust your instincts and prioritize your well-being.

To safeguard against such situations, establish clear, mutually agreed-upon boundaries at the outset of the mentorship. Keep your interactions transparent and aligned with the shared goals of the relationship. If something feels off or crosses a line, it's important to trust your instincts and seek advice from a trusted resource or individual.

Mentorship should always be a source of support, inspiration, and mutual growth. By maintaining clarity, openness, and respect, you can create meaningful relationships that empower you to grow while fostering a safe and constructive environment.

For those interested in exploring this topic further, consider reading *The Gift of Fear* by Gavin de Becker, which provides valuable insights into recognizing and responding to unhealthy or unsafe relationships.

ADVICE FOR MENTORS

Most of this book is geared toward mentees, but I felt it was important to provide advice for mentors in this chapter knowing that some readers fit that category better and also considering that all the mentees reading this book might eventually become mentors themselves and may benefit from knowing this information. (We'll talk more about becoming a mentor in chapter 10.)

Being an advisor or mentor is often about much more than offering career or professional guidance—it's about supporting the whole person. While career success might be the initial focus, a mentee's emotional and mental well-being is just as important. Recognizing this allows mentors to take on a truly transformative role, especially during challenging times.

Imagine you're helping someone navigate a particularly stressful period—perhaps they're trying to balance demanding work and personal commitments, or they're dealing with a personal crisis that's affecting their professional life. While offering advice on managing tasks might help, sometimes what they really need is space to breathe. Encouraging them to prioritize work-life balance, set boundaries, and practice self-care can make a world of difference. These small but meaningful steps can prevent burnout and help them emerge stronger.

One of the most impactful things you can do as a mentor is to create an environment where your mentee feels safe enough to open up. They might be dealing with feelings of overwhelm, anxiety, or uncertainty about their next steps. By keeping the lines of communication open—free from judgment or pressure—you can offer them a vital sense of support. Simple, heartfelt questions like "How are you doing?" or "What's been on your mind lately?" can uncover deeper concerns and help them feel less alone in their struggles.

This is where the principles of servant leadership truly shine. As a servant leader, your role isn't to direct or dictate but to listen, support, and empathize. Instead of immediately jumping to solutions, take the time to understand what your mentee is experiencing—not just in their professional life but in their personal life as well. Maybe they're grappling with self-doubt, a family challenge, or a health concern. By listening without rushing to offer advice, you demonstrate empathy and compassion, which can often be even more valuable than practical guidance. (More on servant leadership in chapter 10.)

THE POWER OF VULNERABILITY IN MENTORSHIP

Sharing your own experiences—whether it's a time when stress overwhelmed you, when things didn't go as planned, or when you leaned on others for support—can be incredibly impactful as a mentor. Being open about your challenges and how you navigated them fosters trust and encourages your mentee to be honest about their own struggles. It's a reminder that no one has it all figured out all the time and that seeking help is a strength, not a weakness. This kind of vulnerability deepens the mentor-mentee relationship, letting them know they don't have to face challenges alone.

At its core, being a mentor is about helping someone develop resilience. Life is full of ups and downs, and one of the greatest gifts you can offer is helping your mentee build the emotional tools to handle adversity. While you're not there to solve every problem, you can guide them in developing skills like emotional intelligence, stress management, and self-reflection—skills that empower them to face future challenges with strength and confidence.

Life can feel heavy at times. We all experience moments where setbacks feel personal, professional challenges seem insurmountable, or the weight of it all becomes overwhelming. As a mentor, you may notice these shifts in your mentee's energy or demeanor—maybe they seem less engaged, more stressed, or just different. These are the moments when a simple check-in can mean the world. Asking, "How are you managing everything?" can open the door to a conversation they didn't realize they needed.

Sometimes, your mentee may be facing challenges that require professional support, like prolonged stress or anxiety. In these moments, gently encouraging them to seek help is one of the most meaningful things you can do. By normalizing therapy or counseling and reinforcing that mental health is as important as physical health, you can help break down barriers that might prevent them from seeking care.

Even when professional help is involved, your role as a steady, supportive presence remains vital. Regular check-ins and words of encouragement remind your mentee of their worth, independent of their productivity or achievements. Your belief in them can help anchor them during difficult times and reaffirm their value, even when they're struggling to see it themselves.

FROM SCREEN TO SERVICE: DOUG JONES AND THE VALUE OF GIVING BACK

Doug Jones, a sci-fi fan favorite, is one of the world's most famous actors who many may not immediately recognize. This is because he often appears on-screen in elaborate costumes or prosthetic makeup, transforming into otherworldly characters. Many journalists have likened him to Lon Chaney, the early movie star famously known as "The Man of a Thousand Faces." Doug has earned a similar moniker for his remarkable roles in films such as *Hellboy, Pan's Labyrinth,* and *The Shape of Water,* which won the Academy Award for Best Picture. He also stars as Saru in *Star Trek*: *Discovery* and has appeared in over twenty-five other films, along with numerous TV programs and commercials.

Doug and his wife, Laurie, have never had children of their own, but over the last thirty years they have mentored dozens of young men and women in the entertainment industry. They've helped these individuals navigate the complexities and challenges of Hollywood, providing moral and emotional guidance in what can be a brutal and unforgiving industry. Doug has been a mentor of mine for many years and provided a sounding board for many of my Hollywood-focused projects. Doug and Laurie have even opened their home to mentees, bringing them in for holidays and, in one instance, formally adopting a young woman they had mentored for many years.

Always modest, Doug rarely speaks publicly about his role as a mentor, but his influence is undeniable. He has been a constant friend, guide, and advisor to countless young professionals in the industry. Beyond his mentorship, Doug is deeply devoted to his fans. He spends an extraordinary amount of time interacting with them online and attending conventions almost every weekend of the year when he's not filming *Star Trek* or working on another project. His tireless engagement has endeared him to fans and friends around the globe.

Doug Jones spreads love wherever he goes. His generosity of spirit and dedication to helping others have not only made him a beloved figure in entertainment but also a shining example of mentorship and servant leadership. He has modeled the value of giving back, inspiring others both on and off the screen.

SUPPORTING THROUGH LIFE'S CHALLENGES

When mentors are serving mentees in the area of mental health or emotional support, there are several key considerations to keep in mind to ensure they offer helpful, empathetic, and appropriate guidance.

Recognize Your Role and Boundaries

- **Know your limits:** Mentors are not mental health professionals. Be aware of the scope of your role and recognize when your mentee may need more specialized support, such as therapy or counseling.
- **Refer when necessary:** If you sense that a mentee's emotional struggles are beyond what you can help with, gently encourage them to seek professional support. It's important to recognize when they need expertise outside of your knowledge.

Create a Supportive Environment

- **Maintain confidentiality:** Ensure that emotional or mental health conversations are treated with respect and privacy. This builds trust and helps mentees feel safe opening up to you.
- **Have a nonjudgmental attitude:** Create an environment where your mentee feels comfortable sharing their feelings or struggles. Approach these conversations without judgment or criticism and focus on being a listener rather than a problem solver.

Listen Actively and Empathetically

- **Be present:** Show up with your full attention, listen carefully, and avoid distractions. This lets your mentee know they are being heard, and that their emotions are valued.

- **Acknowledge their emotions:** Instead of offering solutions immediately, acknowledge their feelings. Statements like "That sounds tough" or "I can understand why you'd feel that way" validate their experiences and show empathy.

Avoid Dismissing Their Feelings

- **Don't minimize struggles:** Even if your mentee's challenges seem small compared to others, never minimize or dismiss their feelings. What may seem like a minor issue to you could be a major source of stress or anxiety for them.
- **Be compassionate, not paternalistic:** Avoid offering clichés like "It could be worse" or "Just think positive." These statements can inadvertently invalidate their feelings or make them feel like they should "get over it."

Encourage Healthy Coping Strategies

- **Promote self-care:** Encourage your mentee to prioritize activities that support their mental health, such as exercise, meditation, journaling, or seeking social support.
- **Help build emotional intelligence:** Guide your mentee in identifying and managing their emotions. Developing emotional intelligence can help

them navigate stressful situations and avoid emotional burnout.

Be Mindful

- **Respect sensitive topics:** Be aware of potential triggers, especially if your mentee has experienced trauma or has mental health conditions like PTSD, depression, or anxiety.
- **Approach sensitive topics carefully:** Avoid pushing them to discuss things they're not ready to talk about.
- **Check in regularly:** Emotional well-being can fluctuate. Checking in periodically lets your mentee know you are concerned about their overall health, not just their performance.

Model Vulnerability

- **Lead by example:** When appropriate, sharing your own experiences with mental health or emotional struggles can help normalize vulnerability and show your mentee that it's okay not to be perfect. This also builds a sense of trust and mutual respect.
- **Be authentic:** Be real about your own emotions and challenges. A mentor who is open about their mental health journey can create a safe space for the mentee to be honest about theirs.

Be Patient

- **Respect their pace:** Mental health challenges are often long-term and complex. Your mentee may need more time to be ready to open up or may take time to work through their feelings. Be patient and avoid pushing them to talk before they're ready.
- **Celebrate small progress:** Acknowledge and celebrate your mentee's small steps toward emotional health, even if they seem minor. This can help build their confidence and reinforce positive change.

Avoid Overwhelming Them with Advice

- **Ask, don't tell:** Instead of offering unsolicited advice, ask open-ended questions like "How do you think you can manage this situation?" or "What's been helping you cope?" This empowers your mentee to take ownership of their well-being and makes them feel more in control.
- **Focus on empowerment:** Your goal as a mentor should be to empower your mentees, not to fix their problems. Help them explore their options and decide on the next best step rather than providing all the answers.

Take Care of Yourself

- **Maintain self-awareness:** Supporting others in their mental health journey can be emotionally taxing. Be mindful of your emotional health and ensure you have outlets for your stress or any emotional impact from these conversations.

- **Seek guidance:** If you find yourself struggling to best support a mentee in this area, don't hesitate to seek guidance from a mental health professional. Having a support network can make you more effective as a mentor.

Help Build a Support Network

- **Encourage broader support:** Remind your mentee that no one person can fulfill all their emotional or mental health needs. Encourage them to build a strong support network of friends, family, professionals, or peer groups that can provide additional care and perspective.
- **Watch for signs of crisis:** While not all mental health struggles are apparent, signs such as withdrawal, drastic mood changes, or mention of self-harm can be indicators that something deeper is going on. If you notice these signs, gently ask if they're okay and provide resources for professional help if necessary.

Mentoring in emotional and mental health requires compassion, patience, and awareness. The most important thing is to be present for your mentee, listen deeply, and offer support in ways that empower them to grow. Remember, your role is to guide, not to fix, and to create a safe, open environment where your mentee feels supported—no matter what mental health challenges they may be facing.

Questions to journal on...

How can your mentors support your emotional and mental well-being beyond career advice, and what areas would you like to discuss with them?

What balance do you seek between professional growth and personal fulfillment, and how can your board help you achieve it?

Chapter Challenge: Consider a time when you had to be of support to someone else in a difficult time. How did you manage?

Instagram, Substack and X @yourboard4life
#chapter8challenge #yourboard4life

CHAPTER 9

NAVIGATING THE GIG ECONOMY WITH A PERSONAL BOARD

- **The new workforce reality:** The gig economy and how having a personal board of directors can provide stability and support in an unpredictable work environment.
- **Strategies for freelancers and gig workers:** Build a board that helps them thrive in nontraditional career paths.

MENTORSHIP AND ACCOUNTABILITY: YOUR KEY TO INDEPENDENT WORK SUCCESS

In today's gig economy, where independent work is increasingly common, building meaningful accountability and mentorship relationships offers both challenges and opportunities for growth.

The first step is identifying your needs and seeking out resources or communities that align with your goals. Online platforms, professional networks, and mentorship programs are excellent starting points for connecting with individuals who can provide guidance and support. Whether it's finding a mentor with years of experience or an accountability partner facing similar challenges, these relationships form the bedrock of personal and professional development.

Clarity and communication are essential to fostering effective mentorship and accountability. Clearly defining your goals and setting expectations helps create purposeful relationships that are mutually beneficial. Sharing your objectives—whether focused on skill-building, career growth, or balancing work and life—enables mentors and partners to offer tailored advice and support. Regular check-ins, whether through virtual meetings or progress updates, keep everyone aligned and create a sense of shared commitment.

For many, accountability relationships thrive best within a community. Joining or creating peer groups offers a platform for sharing experiences, exchanging ideas, and celebrating successes. These groups provide not only practical advice and encouragement but also a sense of camaraderie that counters the isolation often associated with solo work. In these collaborative spaces, individuals grow not only by receiving support but also by offering their insights to others.

Consistency and self-reflection play crucial roles in making these relationships impactful. Prioritizing regular interaction, staying open to feedback, and following through on commitments help build trust and momentum. Taking time to celebrate achievements and reflect on lessons learned reinforces the value of these connections and keeps the focus on continued growth.

FROM ISOLATION TO OPPORTUNITY

The gig economy brings unparalleled freedom, but it also requires self-discipline and a proactive approach to building support systems. By intentionally fostering a network of mentors, accountability partners, and supportive peers, professionals can confidently navigate the complexities of independent work. These relationships transform challenges into opportunities, providing the structure and encouragement needed for lasting success.

Here are some strategies to help you cultivate these relationships effectively:

Leverage Online Platforms

- **Join professional networks:** Join platforms like LinkedIn, Upwork, or specialized forums related to your field. Engage in discussions, share your work, and connect with others.
- **Use mentorship platforms:** Use sites like MentorCruise, SCORE, or micro-mentorship platforms where you can find mentors tailored to your specific needs and goals.

Set Clear Goals and Expectations

- **Define your objectives:** Clearly outline your goals through mentorship and accountability. This could be skill development, career advice, or networking.
- **Communicate your needs:** When reaching out to potential mentors or accountability partners, be specific about your goals and how they can support you.

Build a Supportive Community

- **Join local or virtual meetups:** Attend industry events, workshops, or webinars where you can meet like-minded professionals. Platforms like Meetup.com can help you find relevant gatherings.

- **Create or join peer groups:** Form small groups with fellow gig workers where you can share experiences, challenges, and successes. Regular check-ins can foster accountability.

Establish Regular Check-Ins

- **Schedule meetings:** Set up regular meetings with your mentor or accountability partner, whether monthly or bimonthly (for example). Consistent interaction helps maintain focus and motivation.
- **Use video calls:** If in-person meetings aren't feasible, utilize video conferencing tools to connect, as face-to-face communication can strengthen relationships.

Utilize Accountability Tools

- **Use goal-tracking apps:** Use tools like Trello, Asana, or Todoist to track your progress and share it with your accountability partner.
- **Provide progress reports:** Share periodic updates on your goals and challenges with your mentor, allowing for constructive feedback and guidance.

Be Open to Feedback

- **Embrace constructive criticism:** Be receptive to feedback from your mentor or accountability partner. This openness can lead to personal and professional growth.

- **Ask questions:** Encourage your mentor to provide insights on your work, decisions, and areas for improvement. This dialogue can deepen your relationship and enhance your learning.

Reciprocate and Support Others

- **Offer your expertise:** As you build your knowledge and experience, look for opportunities to mentor others in your network. This reciprocity can strengthen connections.
- **Share resources:** Help your accountability partner or mentor by sharing valuable resources, articles, or contacts in your industry.

Stay Committed and Consistent

- **Prioritize relationships:** Treat your mentorship and accountability relationships as essential commitments. Try to nurture them regularly.
- **Follow through on actions:** Hold yourself accountable for the tasks or goals you set with your mentor or partner. Consistency fosters trust and respect in these relationships.

Reflect on Progress

- **Perform regular self-assessments:** Take time to reflect on your growth and challenges. Consider what's working and what could improve in your mentorship and accountability relationships.

- **Celebrate milestones:** Acknowledge and celebrate your achievements, no matter how small. Sharing these moments with your mentor can strengthen your bond.

FROM MENTEE TO MENTOR: ALEX'S JOURNEY

To illustrate, consider a freelance writer named Alex, who loved the flexibility of writing for different clients but often struggled with self-discipline and long-term career planning. Realizing the importance of mentorship and accountability, Alex started by exploring online communities and forums related to freelance writing. He joined platforms like Medium, where he published his work and interacted with other writers and editors. During one such interaction, he discovered a professional organization for freelance writers, which provided resources and mentorship programs. Motivated by this discovery, Alex signed up and connected with an experienced editor who became his mentor.

With mentorship in place, Alex set clear goals for the relationship. He wanted to improve his writing craft, better understand the business side of freelancing, and learn strategies for building long-term client relationships. When reaching out to his mentor, he communicated his aspirations openly and asked for guidance tailored to his unique situation.

Understanding the power of community, Alex didn't stop at mentorship. He attended online and in-person writing workshops where he met fellow freelancers. Inspired by the energy and mutual support, Alex formed a small accountability group with three other writers. They decided to meet virtually every two weeks to discuss their progress, share advice, and keep each other motivated.

To maintain momentum, Alex scheduled regular one-on-one sessions with his mentor. These monthly video calls allowed him to seek feedback on his writing and discuss strategies for acquiring high-value clients. Alex prepared thoroughly for each session, bringing specific questions and examples of his work. His mentor's constructive criticism and industry insights were instrumental in shaping Alex's career path.

To keep himself on track between sessions, Alex used project management tools like Asana to outline his goals and monitor his progress. He shared updates with his mentor and accountability group, fostering an environment of mutual trust and encouragement. This transparency helped Alex stay focused and motivated.

Embracing the value of feedback, Alex developed a mindset of continuous improvement. He welcomed his mentor's advice and used it as an opportunity to refine his craft. With time, Alex also began sharing his expertise, offering his accountability group tips and resources. This act of giving back strengthened his confidence and enriched his relationships within the group.

Alex was committed to maintaining and growing these relationships. He prioritized his check-ins, followed through on commitments, and consciously showed gratitude to his mentor and peers. By doing so, he built a network rooted in trust and mutual respect.

Regular self-reflection became an integral part of Alex's journey. He tracked his achievements, identified areas for growth, and celebrated his milestones. Each accomplishment—finishing a challenging project or landing a new client—was shared with his mentor and accountability group, reinforcing the value of their support.

Through his dedication to building meaningful connections, Alex transformed his solo freelancing experience into a collaborative and empowering journey. By embracing accountability and actively seeking mentorship, he improved his skills, expanded his network, and found a sense of belonging in the gig economy. Alex learned that even in a world of independent work, collaboration and mentorship are invaluable tools for success.

Although many claim to have mentors, they rely solely on social media influencers or online content creators for guidance. While these resources can provide valuable insights, they lack the personal touch required for proper accountability. Influencers cannot engage directly with your unique circumstances or provide tailored advice.

I encourage you to prioritize building in-person relationships. These connections offer the most prosperous opportunities to maximize the benefits of mentorship and accountability, ensuring a more personalized and impactful experience.

Questions to journal on...

How can a mentor help you navigate the unique challenges of the gig economy, such as uncertainty and instability?

How can you move from the online mentorship community to an in-person one?

Chapter Challenge: What specific skills or perspectives do you seek from mentors to thrive in a nontraditional career path?

Instagram, Substack and X @yourboard4life
#chapter9challenge #yourboard4life

CHAPTER 10

GIVING BACK—BECOMING A BOARD MENTOR FOR OTHERS

- **Paying it forward:** Give back by serving as mentors to others. The personal and professional rewards of mentoring can enhance one's own life and career.
- **Serving your mentors:** Continue to serve existing mentors or board members, creating a cycle of support and growth. Servant leadership is key.
- **Adapting your board:** Regularly reassess and evolve your board as life and career progress. Goals change; new mentors may be needed.

THE JOY OF MENTORSHIP

Mentoring others has been one of the most rewarding experiences of my life. I've been fortunate to learn from so many remarkable mentors, and being able to give back in a similar way feels both fulfilling and meaningful. Since starting my own business in 2000, I've welcomed interns nearly every semester or quarter, making myself available to guide and support them. Each experience has been unique and rewarding, and I've always sought to mentor as many people as possible.

Many of these students have gone on to pursue exciting opportunities, and many have remained in touch and continued our mentorship relationships over the years. Some of these relationships have grown into valuable friendships. I genuinely enjoy sharing my experiences and expertise, particularly with young people, as I see it as a way to inspire and empower the next generation.

My approach to mentorship and leadership is deeply rooted in the philosophy of servant leadership, which I've mentioned earlier in this book but want to explore in greater depth here.

SERVANT LEADERSHIP: LEADING THROUGH SERVICE

Servant leadership is a philosophy that places service to others at the core of leadership. Rather than prioritizing personal ambition or exerting control, a servant leader focuses on supporting the growth, well-being, and empowerment of those they lead. This approach stems from the belief that true leadership involves creating an environment where individuals and communities can thrive. By prioritizing service over personal gain or organizational power, servant leaders foster a culture of collaboration, trust, and mutual respect.

For me, servant leadership means leading with empathy and integrity. It's about actively listening to others, understanding their needs, and finding ways to help them succeed. Whether it's guiding an intern through a new project or offering advice on career decisions, my goal is to empower those I mentor to grow into confident, capable individuals who can achieve their own goals and make a difference in the world.

Mentorship, at its heart, is about connection, encouragement, and shared learning. It's an opportunity not only to teach but also to learn, and it has enriched my life in ways I never could have imagined. I hope that by embracing the principles of servant leadership, you can continue to inspire and support others on their journeys—just as my mentors have done for me.

Important aspects of servant leadership include:

- **Empathy and Listening:** Servant leaders prioritize understanding their team members' needs and concerns. They actively listen, show genuine interest in others' perspectives, and strive to see situations from others' points of view. This empathetic approach helps build trust and create strong, supportive relationships.
- **Empowering Others:** Servant leaders seek to empower and uplift those around them by giving them the tools, resources, and confidence they need to succeed. They focus on developing their team's skills, knowledge, and abilities and encourage personal and professional growth.
- **Fostering Community and Collaboration:** Servant leaders value the importance of collaboration and encourage a sense of community within their teams or organizations. They foster an environment of inclusivity and teamwork, recognizing that collective effort often yields better results than individual pursuits.
- **Humility:** Servant leaders lead with humility, acknowledging that they don't have all the answers and that their role is to guide and support others rather than command them. They are willing to

admit mistakes, learn from them, and give credit where it's due.

- **Ethical Decision-Making:** Servant leadership is deeply rooted in ethical behavior and a strong sense of responsibility toward others. Decisions focus on what suits the people and communities affected, even if they don't align with short-term organizational goals.
- **Stewardship:** Servant leaders see themselves as stewards of the person, organization, or group they lead. This means they take responsibility for the long-term well-being of the people and resources in their care. Stewardship involves making decisions that benefit not just the organization but also individuals.
- **Commitment to the Growth of Others:** Servant leaders actively contribute to their team members' personal and professional development. This commitment goes beyond focusing on tasks and goals—it also includes helping others achieve personal fulfillment and find purpose in their work.
- **Building a Shared Vision:** Servant leaders work to inspire and align individuals and their teams around a common purpose. They emphasize shared goals and values, ensuring everyone understands their contribution to the broader mission and feels motivated to pursue collective success.

WHY SERVANT LEADERSHIP MATTERS

The servant leadership approach fosters long-term commitment, loyalty, and a sense of belonging among individuals, teams, or organizations.

Some of history's most influential figures, such as **Jesus of Nazareth** and **Nelson Mandela,** exemplify servant leadership through their dedication to serving others and improving the world. They demonstrated empathy, empowered others, and prioritized justice and community well-being.

One particularly profound example of servant leadership comes from the story of Jesus washing the feet of his followers—a task typically reserved for household servants. By performing this act, Jesus challenged cultural norms and conveyed a powerful message: True leadership isn't about wielding power or authority but about serving others with humility and care. This meaningful gesture encouraged his followers to lead by example, placing others' needs above their own.

Jesus also highlighted the importance of personal growth and forgiveness in leadership. When his followers faltered—such as Peter denying him—Jesus responded with understanding and compassion. Rather than chastising Peter, he reassured him of his worth and role within the community. This example shows how effective leaders support and uplift others, even in moments of failure, fostering resilience and growth.

Nelson Mandela's life offers a modern blueprint for servant leadership. During his twenty-seven years of imprisonment, Mandela remained steadfast in his vision for a united South Africa. Rather than allowing bitterness to consume him, he used his time to reflect and develop a leadership style centered on reconciliation and healing. Upon his release, Mandela emphasized forgiveness, collaboration, and understanding, inspiring a nation to move toward unity.

His decision to serve only one term as president exemplified his selflessness and commitment to the greater good. By prioritizing the country's stability over personal ambition, Mandela demonstrated that leadership is about empowering others and ensuring a brighter future for all.

In the realm of mentorship, Mandela's legacy teaches us that impactful mentors lead by example, offering guidance with patience, sacrifice, and a focus on helping others realize their potential. His ability to listen, even to those who opposed him, fostered understanding and bridged divides.

Mandela's approach reminds us that mentorship isn't about asserting authority but about walking alongside those we guide. By putting others first and embodying integrity and resilience, mentors can inspire meaningful, transformative change in individuals and communities alike. His life serves as a timeless testament to the profound impact of servant leadership.

FROM KITCHEN TO KINDNESS: WILL GUIDARA'S "UNREASONABLE" LEADERSHIP

A more contemporary example is **Will Guidara,** who has exemplified this approach.

Will's story is a testament to the transformative power of putting others first—a philosophy he has applied not just in hospitality but also in leadership and mentorship. As the co-owner of a Michelin three-star restaurant, Eleven Madison Park, Guidara helped shape one of the most iconic restaurants in the world, leading it to earn the title of the World's Best Restaurant in 2017. But his achievements go far beyond accolades. At the heart of

Guidara's success is his belief in what he calls "unreasonable hospitality"—the idea that going above and beyond for others, even in the smallest ways, can create extraordinary results.

In his book *Unreasonable Hospitality: The Remarkable Power of Giving People More Than They Expect,* Guidara shares how this mindset not only defines the way he treats guests but also how he leads his team. For him, hospitality isn't just about service—it is about human connection. He understands that people thrive when they feel seen, valued, and cared for. Whether it is creating unforgettable moments for guests or empowering his staff to take ownership of their roles, his approach is always rooted in generosity and empathy.

This philosophy is deeply intertwined with the principles of servant leadership, which Guidara embodies in everything he does. Like a servant leader, Guidara prioritizes the needs of others—whether they are a diner, an employee, or a mentee. He believes that leadership is not about commanding but about serving, and that true impact comes from uplifting those around you.

For Guidara, even the smallest gestures matter. He often tells stories of how tiny, thoughtful acts—like giving a guest a personalized note or arranging a surprise experience—creates moments that people cherish for years. These actions weren't grand or costly, but they were deeply personal. Similarly, in mentorship, it's often the small, intentional efforts that make the biggest difference: A kind word, a thoughtful piece of advice, or a meaningful introduction can be life-changing for someone trying to find their way.

Listening is another cornerstone of Guidara's approach. At Eleven Madison Park, he makes it a point to listen—not just to guests, but to his team. By understanding their perspectives, he creates an environment where people feel empowered to make decisions and contribute meaningfully. This lesson translates seamlessly into mentorship. A good mentor listens deeply, understanding not only a mentee's goals but also their fears, challenges, and untapped potential. It's through this understanding that mentors can provide personalized guidance that truly resonates.

Guidara's generosity extends beyond his restaurant walls. He cofounded the Welcome Conference, an annual event designed to bring leaders from across industries together to share ideas and inspire one another. The event reflects of his belief that generosity and collaboration are keys to meaningful leadership. It's not about holding on to power or influence but about using it to lift others up.

One of the more complex lessons Guidara touches on is the tension between achieving goals and staying true to one's values. In *Unreasonable Hospitality*, he acknowledges that some might argue for compromising ethics to secure success, but he firmly rejects this idea. For him, the journey is just as important as the destination. The decisions you make along the way—the small, seemingly inconsequential choices—define not only the outcome but also the integrity of your character. This is a powerful lesson for mentors, who often serve as moral compasses for those they guide. Guidara's story reminds us that how we achieve success matters just as much as achieving it.

Ultimately, Will Guidara's life and philosophy serve as a master class in servant leadership. He has shown that generosity, empathy, and an unwavering commitment to others can create not only exceptional experiences but also lasting impact. For mentors, his lessons are clear: Listen deeply, act with intention, and always prioritize the growth and well-being of those you lead. Whether you're guiding a mentee or serving a team, the principles of "unreasonable hospitality" are a powerful way to model mentorship and leadership with heart.

TOUGH MENTORSHIPS AND DEMANDING BOSSES

Serving your mentors is a concept I emphasize in this book, as it's essential to building a truly reciprocal relationship. While mentorship often involves the mentor providing guidance, advice, and support, it's essential for mentees to also consider ways to give back and serve their mentors. A strong mentor-mentee relationship should never be a one-way street. Instead, it should be a dynamic partnership where learning and support flow in both directions.

On rare occasions, however, you could end up with a challenging mentorship connection, such as a difficult boss. Being a good employee and a servant leader to someone who is both your boss, and a powerful, demanding individual requires learning certain key lessons:

- **Humility:** Serving others, even those who are difficult or unappreciative, is an essential skill. Many of the most impactful roles in life require working with people who are complex or challenging, and fulfilling these roles offers the greatest potential to influence others, your field, or even the world.
- **Patience and Emotional Resilience:** You learn to prioritize your goals and purpose above your emotions and ego, which is critical in high-stakes or high-pressure environments.

The Devil Is in the Details

I once had a mentor who was also a client. She was an Emmy-winning actress and challenged me in many ways. She was intense, highly demanding, a perfectionist, and not one to praise very often. I would compare her to the fictional character Miranda Priestly from *The Devil Wears Prada.* She was very high-maintenance and one of several clients I've worked for who shared these traits.

Whenever I speak to young people or college students, I recommend watching *The Devil Wears Prada.* It offers many valuable lessons that, if applied, can make you indispensable and an asset to any employer. It also teaches the critical skill of managing your boss. In fact, there are books on this very topic.

- **Problem-Solving Under Pressure:** Extreme demands often push you to find solutions you might not have otherwise discovered. This stretching of your abilities leads to growth and innovation.
- **Understanding Expectations:** High-level professionals have specific expectations for your work product and professionalism. Once you understand these, the job becomes more manageable. Over time, you'll develop the foresight and conscientiousness to anticipate your boss's needs, often exceeding their expectations. When you reach this point, the work becomes more enjoyable and even fun—almost like a game.
- **Building Trust:** By consistently performing well and succeeding under pressure, you build a high level of trust with your boss or mentor. Although it's tempting to quit when you feel unap

preciated or overwhelmed, I encourage sticking it out. Grow where you are planted and take on the challenge. You'll learn a lot about yourself in the process. In my experience, enduring these challenges often leads to long-term relationships with those mentors/bosses, and they tend to soften over time.

(See the books I recommended below here.)

It's Okay to Manage Your Boss: The Step-by-Step Program for Making the Best of Your Most Important Relationship at Work by Bruce Tulgan

Managing Up: How to Move Up, Win at Work, and Succeed with Any Type of Boss by Mary Abbajay

Additional resources worth reading are the books *Managing Your Manager: How to Get Ahead with Any Type of Boss* by Gonzague Dufour and *How to Lead When Your Boss Can't (or Won't)* by John C. Maxwell.

That said, serving others doesn't mean you should compromise your values or boundaries or be a doormat. If you're ever asked to do something illegal or immoral, you should absolutely refuse and exercise your rights. And sometimes the working relationship is just plain toxic and you need to move on. Those instances notwithstanding (or aside from those scenarios), I advocate for doing what your boss asks, even if it's outside your job description. This attitude can make you all but irreplaceable.

WHERE MENTORSHIP MEETS UNEXPECTED REWARDS

A memorable outcome from my time with the actress mentor/ client: I had mentioned to her in passing that I was a fan of the ABC TV show *Alias* and had a small crush on the star, Jennifer Garner. My mentor, being well-connected as a successful actress, pulled some strings. To my surprise, she arranged for me to visit the set of *Alias,* where I not only met Jennifer Garner but also appeared as a featured extra playing a CIA agent in the second-season finale. It was an incredible reward for a job well done and remains a cherished memory. It was slow in coming but was a demonstration of her respect for me and appreciation for my work and is a great example of the sort of unintended benefits of serving your mentors well.

For many mentees, it can be challenging to identify how to be of service to someone more experienced or accomplished. However, one area where mentees can often provide valuable support is by sharing their knowledge of technology, trends, and social media. Many older mentors may feel less comfortable navigating new technologies, digital tools, or trends in social media. If you're a younger mentee, offering to help your mentor understand these tools—or even set up and manage things like social media profiles or video conferencing platforms—can be an efficient and meaningful way to give back.

Beyond these examples, being available and letting your mentor know you're willing to help in any way can open the door to unexpected opportunities to serve. You might be able to offer advice or a fresh perspective on a challenge they're facing, share insights into trends in your industry or community, or simply provide encouragement when they need it most. Sometimes, being a sounding board for their ideas or offering to assist with a project can make a real difference.

Remember, mentorship is about growth—for both parties. As a mentee, don't underestimate the value you bring to the relationship. Your unique experiences, skills, and outlook can be just as enriching for your mentor as their wisdom and guidance are for you. Some of the most impactful lessons I've learned have come not from my mentors but from my mentees and the people I've worked with over the years.

Ultimately, serving your mentor strengthens the relationship and creates a deeper connection, fostering trust, mutual respect, and shared growth. By approaching the relationship with a spirit of generosity and collaboration, you'll find that the benefits of mentorship become even more prosperous and rewarding for you and your mentor.

PAYING IT FORWARD

Serving your mentor doesn't stop with them—it extends to the broader idea of paying it forward. Embracing a mindset of service means understanding that the lessons, guidance, and wisdom you've received are meant to be shared. Mentorship is about creating a ripple effect; what your mentor has invested in you should inspire you to invest in others. By mentoring, you're not only sharing knowledge—you're continuing the cycle of humility, service, and growth.

I mentioned earlier that one of my earliest professional mentors was a state legislator I met during my first year of college. Witnessing his dedication to his constituents confirmed to me that he was a genuine public servant. Although our political views differed, I saw many admirable qualities in him and valued maintaining a connection. Our personalities aligned well, and over the years, we stayed in touch. Eventually, I had the privilege of mentoring his son. His parents expressed heartfelt gratitude, and being able to give back in this way was incredibly fulfilling.

Mentoring others is also about leading by example. Through mentorship, you reflect the values your mentors instilled in you—patience, generosity, and a commitment to helping others. In doing so, you honor their guidance while fostering a culture of service and leadership. Each act of mentorship—whether offering advice, lending an ear, or helping someone chart their path—contributes to a legacy of mutual growth and empowerment.

At its core, mentorship is about relationships that go beyond simple transactions. Approaching mentorship with a mindset of service transforms it into a meaningful exchange built on mutual respect, support, and shared growth.

RECOGNIZING WHEN TO PIVOT THE RELATIONSHIP

As your career evolves, so too might your mentorship relationships. There may come a time when regular meetings are no longer necessary, or your needs for guidance shift. Transitioning a mentorship when the time is right allows both mentor and mentee to grow independently while preserving the connection for future collaboration.

Even if regular guidance isn't needed anymore, staying connected keeps the door open for future advice or support. It's natural for some mentorships to conclude or evolve as goals are achieved and professional priorities change. Recognizing when to adapt or step back from a mentorship is part of the process, but this doesn't mean the relationship has to end.

Adding mentors as you progress into different projects, endeavors, or careers in your life is essential. Keep the pipeline open and go through the process I've outlined in this book to seek out and add more mentors to your board, as needed. This is not a one-and-done situation; it may be something you revisit every few years or so. I am still emphasizing that you need to stay connected and engage in long-term relationships with your mentors. This is not about creating short-term situations but stakeholders in your future and a long-term strategy.

Sustaining relationships, however, requires effort and care. Much like tending a garden, relationships need regular attention to thrive. Neglecting them may lead to missed opportunities when you need support later. By nurturing these connections, you ensure they remain strong and valuable long-term. The effort is worth it, and the rewards will be long-lasting—I can confidently promise you that!

Knowing When It's Time to Pivot

You might notice that a mentorship needs to shift when:

- You've reached the goals that initially brought you to your mentor.
- Your career has taken a turn where you need different kinds of advice.
- Your check-ins have become less frequent, and that feels natural.
- Your mentor's expertise isn't as directly relevant to your current path.

Instead of seeing this as the end of the mentorship, think of it as an evolution. *Relationships don't have to dissolve just because they change.*

Keeping the Connection Without the Formality

If you don't need regular meetings anymore, you can still maintain the relationship in ways that feel organic:

- **Express appreciation:** A quick note saying, "Your advice on X really helped me, and I just wanted to say thank you again!" goes a long way.
- **Check in occasionally:** A simple message, an invite to an event, or even a comment on something they've shared online can keep the connection warm.
- **Find ways to give back:** As you grow, there may be ways you can support your mentor—whether that's making introductions, offering insights, or just being a great connection for them.
- **Stay on their radar:** Keep them in the loop on milestones, career updates, or projects they might find interesting.

Adding New Mentors as You Grow

Your board of mentors is something you can keep building as your career evolves. Each stage of life may require different guidance, so:

- **Check in with yourself every few years:** Are there areas where you could use new perspectives? Is there someone in your network you admire who could be a great mentor?
- **Lean on your existing mentors for connections:** Often, they know just the right people to introduce you to.

- **Mix it up:** Having mentors from different industries, backgrounds, and experiences gives you a well-rounded support system.

Keeping Long-Term Mentorships Strong

Good mentorships shouldn't feel transactional—they're relationships that can last a lifetime if you put in the effort. To keep them going:

- **Stay in touch, even when you don't "need" something:** A quick "hello" keeps the relationship alive.
- **Let them know their advice still resonates:** Sharing how their guidance has impacted you over time shows them their mentorship mattered.
- **Give back when you can:** Whether it's sharing a resource, making an introduction, or supporting their work, a little reciprocity goes a long way.

FINAL THOUGHT ON PIVOTING

Mentorships aren't meant to be rigid. They evolve, just like we do. By staying in touch, knowing when to pivot, and continuing to build your network, you'll always have trusted advisors in your corner—ready to support you when you need them.

Question to journal on...

How can you serve as a mentor to others, and what lessons can you share?

Chapter Challenge: What steps can you take to express gratitude and support to your mentors, creating a cycle of growth and mentorship?

Instagram, Substack and X @yourboard4life
#chapter10challenge #yourboard4life

CONCLUSION

A LIFELONG DANCE

MENTORSHIP IS NOT A NEW concept; it has been a cornerstone of cultures around the world for centuries. However, in recent decades, its prominence has waned due to the dispersion of families and the diminishing role of traditional social and cultural networks. As people move away from their roots, they often leave behind the natural support systems that once nurtured mentorship and community.

Today, we've become more transactional and less relational. Despite having countless ways to connect through technology, many people long for the supportive systems of the past, systems that seem increasingly out of reach.

Over the years, I've been fortunate to meet and work with many extraordinary individuals—from world leaders and Nobel Prize winners to renowned journalists, athletes, entertainers, and tech industry pioneers. While I can't share all my stories out of respect for privacy and confidentiality, one consistent theme among them is the profound role mentorship has played in their lives. Nearly all of them attribute a portion of their success to the mentors who guided them along the way.

The truth is that no one achieves great success entirely on their own. The most accomplished people recognize the importance of relationships, of learning from others, and of giving back to those whose footsteps they have followed.

So, how do we create success—both personal and professional? By being intentional about building and maintaining mentorships. It requires effort, discipline, and patience, but the rewards are immeasurable. Meaningful relationships don't just happen by chance; they take intention and commitment.

I hope the stories and insights in this book have helped highlight the value of mentorship and inspired you to take the first step in building your own Board of Directors for Life. As you begin this journey, you may find it challenging at first, but eventually it will feel more natural and fulfilling. These relationships will enrich your life in ways you may not yet imagine and will help you grow into the person you aspire to be.

Creating a diverse group of mentors, rather than relying on just one, is a unique approach that I believe will make a significant difference as you progress in life. This decision has been one of the most impactful of my own life, and I hope it inspires you to embrace mentorship as a way to not only transform your life but also positively influence the lives of those around you.

Together, we can foster a culture where mentorship flourishes once again—building connections, sharing wisdom, and ensuring that no one has to navigate life's challenges alone.

Feel free to share your journey! Go to my website, www.yourboard4life.com, or social media accounts @yourboard4life on Instagram, Substack or X where I will have more stories to share and where you can tell us your story, ask for advice, or simply connect about your experience as a mentor or mentee.

BIBLIOGRAPHY

Baron, Tony. *The Art of Servant Leadership: Designing Your Organization for the Sake of Others*. New York: Wheatmark, 2010.

Bible. English Standard Version. Proverbs 15:22, Acts 9:26-27, Acts 11:22-26, Acts 13

Blanchard, Ken, and Phil Hodges. *Servant Leader: Transforming Your Heart, Head, Hands and Habits*. Nashville: Thomas Nelson, 2003.

Briggs Myers, Isabel, and Peter B. Myers. *Gifts Differing: Understanding Personality Type*. Sunnyvale: CPP, 1995.

Brown, Brené. *Dare to Lead: Brave Work. Tough Conversations. Whole Hearts*. New York: Random House, 2018.

Clear, James. *Atomic Habits: An Easy & Proven Way to Build Good Habits & Break Bad Ones*. New York: Avery, 2018.

Dennison, Kara. "The Power of Mentorship: How Mentors Can Help Employees Grow and Succeed." *Forbes*, March 27, 2023. https://www.forbes.com/sites/karadennison/2023/03/27/the-power-of-mentorship-how-mentors-can-help-employees-grow-and-succeed/.

Doug Jones, interview with author.

Dungy, Tony. *The Mentor Leader: Secrets to Building People and Teams That Win Consistently*. Carol Stream, IL: Tyndale Momentum, 2011.

Frankel, David, dir. *The Devil Wears Prada*. 20th Century Fox, 2006.

Geoffreys, Clayton. *Stephen Curry: The Inspiring Story of One of Basketball's Sharpest Shooters*. Independently published, 2022.

Gilbert, Martin. *Churchill: A Life*. New York: Henry Holt and Company, 1991.

Goodwin, Doris Kearns. *The Fitzgeralds and the Kennedys: An American Saga*. New York: Simon & Schuster, 1987.

Goodwin, Doris Kearns. *Team of Rivals: The Political Genius of Abraham Lincoln*. New York: Simon & Schuster, 2006.

Goleman, Daniel. *Emotional Intelligence: Why It Can Matter More Than IQ*. New York: Bantam, 2005.

Guidara, Will. *Unreasonable Hospitality: The Remarkable Power of Giving People More Than They Expect*. New York: Optimism Press, 2022.

Hammond, John S., Ralph L. Keeney, and Howard Raiffa. *Smart Choices: A Practical Guide to Making Better Decisions*. Brighton, MA: Harvard Business Review Press, 2015.

Homer. *The Odyssey*. Translated by Robert Fagles. New York: Penguin Books, 1996.

Hougaard, Rasmus, and Jacqueline Carter. "Becoming a More Humane Leader." *Harvard Business Review*, November 23, 2021. https://hbr.org/2021/11/becoming-a-more-humane-leader.Ingersoll, Fred. "The History of Apprenticeship: From Ancient Civilizations to Modern Times." LinkedIn, July 10, 2024. https://www.linkedin.com/pulse/history-apprenticeship-from-ancient-civilizations-dr-fred-4gfuc/.

Ishizaka, Alessio, and Philippe Nemery. *Multi-Criteria Decision Analysis: Methods and Software*. New York: Wiley, 2013.

Ireland, Kathy, and Laura Morton. *Powerful Inspirations: Eight Lessons That Will Change Your Life*. New York: Doubleday, 2002.

Isaacson, Walter. *Steve Jobs*. New York: Simon & Schuster, 2011.

James, Steve. *Stephen Curry: A Sharpshooter's Journey to the NBA & Beyond*. Independently published, 2016.

Janis, Irving L. *Groupthink: Psychological Studies of Policy Decisions and Fiascoes*. Boston, MA: Cengage Learning, 1982.

Jenkins, Roy. *Churchill: A Biography*. New York: Farrar, Straus and Giroux, 2001.

Josephson, Matthew. *Edison: A Biography*. New York: History Book Club, 2003.

Kuchera, Ben. "Loving Doug Jones, the Invisible Movie Star from *Hellboy* and *Shape of Water*." *Polygon*, January 23, 2018. https://www.polygon.com/2018/1/23/16923122/doug-jones-shape-of-water-oscar.

Laughlin, Fredric L., and Robert C. Andringa. *Good Governance for Nonprofits: Developing Principles and Policies for an Effective Board*. New York: AMACOM Books, 2007.

Lowenstein, Roger. *Buffett: The Making of an American Capitalist*. New York: Penguin Books, 2008.

Mandela, Nelson. *Long Walk to Freedom: The Autobiography of Nelson Mandela*. New York: Back Bay Books, 1995.

Morse, Gardiner. "The Science Behind Six Degrees." *Harvard Business Review*, February 2003. https://hbr.org/2003/02/the-science-behind-six-degrees.

Ohno, Apolo. *Hard Pivot: Embrace Change. Find Purpose. Show Up Fully*. Louisville, CO: Sounds True, 2022.

Ohno, Apolo. *Zero Regrets: Be Greater Than Yesterday*. New York: Atria, 2010.

O'Neill, Gerard. *Rogues and Redeemers: When Politics Was King in Irish Boston*. New York: Crown Publishing, 2012.

Pegg, Mike. *The Art of Mentoring: How You Can Be a Superb Mentor*. Lake Charles, LA: Global Management Enterprises, 2011.

Project Management Experts, LLC. "Emotional Intelligence: A Skill All Project Managers Can Learn." Project Management Experts, November 26, 2019. https://www.projectmanagementexperts.com/emotional-intelligence-a-skill-all-project-managers-can-learn/.

Roberts, Andrew. *Churchill: Walking with Destiny*. New York: Viking, 2018.

Schlender, Brent, and Rick Tetzeli. *Becoming Steve Jobs: The Evolution of a Reckless Upstart into a Visionary Leader.* New York: Crown, 2015.

Schroeder, Alice. *The Snowball: Warren Buffett and the Business of Life.* New York: Bantam Books, 2008.

Sinek, Simon, David Mead, and Peter Docker. *Find Your Why: A Practical Guide for Discovering Purpose for You and Your Team.* New York: Portfolio, 2017.

Watts, Alan. *The Book: On the Taboo Against Knowing Who You Are.* New York: Pantheon, 1966.

Wheatley, Margaret J. *Leadership and the New Science: Discovering Order in a Chaotic World.* New York: Berrett-Koehler, 2006.

ACKNOWLEDGMENTS

I WANT TO THANK THE mentors who have helped to shape me over the years by name. They were generous in giving me their time, knowledge, and hard-earned experience: Daniel O'Connor, Honorable John Robinson, John Michler, Stan Staples, Dr. Stephen Portch, San Orr Jr., Dr. George Newtown, Dr. Angela Burger, Honorable Alan Amos, Harold Larson, Barbara Greenleaf, and Isabelle Finney.

I want to thank my friends who acted as editors and advisors or who assisted in some way to make this book happen: Lesa Stern, Kurt Gabriel, Barbara Greenleaf, Wendy Whitman, Monica Mallett, Laura Hassan, Truman Denney, and Brian Hoffmann. Also, I want to thank my graphic designer, Brian Buffon.

And I'd like to thank Post Hill Press and its publisher, Anthony Ziccardi, for believing in the book and for publishing it.

ABOUT THE AUTHOR

Photo Credit: Brian Buffon

DENNIS BAKER, CEO OF DM Baker Media Relations, is an innovative leader with expertise in media messaging, crisis management, and technology innovation. He has raised millions for nonprofits, supporting causes such as museums, hospitals, universities, and international aid organizations. As a PR expert, Baker has managed campaigns for *New York Times* bestselling authors, advocacy groups, and entertainers.

Founder of Polis Assist, a mobile app for fee-free parking in major cities, Baker has earned recognition as a finalist in the Dr. Patrick Soon-Shiong Innovation Awards and Leading Cities AcceliCITY program, voted number 2 of the top 10 best apps by *LA Weekly*. A graduate of Westmont College and a Hansard Scholar at the London School of Economics, he has worked for the US Senate, the British House of Commons, and FOX-TV. Baker serves on multiple human rights nonprofit boards, including EPIC Impact Society, and is part of the Nexus Summit community.